Short Role-playing Simulations for World History Classrooms

By Richard Di Giacomo
1st Edition © 1999
2nd Edition © 2000
3rd Edition © 2003

The licensing for this book includes the right for one teacher to reproduce as many copies of the student handouts as needed for his or her students and a single set of copies of the teacher instructions for personal use. A single copy of this book may be shared in a department, but if it is to be used at more than one school site, or at district curriculum library, or other facility, each site should purchase its own copies.

ISBN 0-9706237-0-4

Acknowledgements

I would like to dedicate this book to Donald Gregory of Gregory Publications for encouraging me to someday publish books of my own. I would like to thank Diane Hart for all of her helpful suggestions for revisions and for helping me to market this book. I would also like to thank Aaron Willis and others at Social Studies School Service for helping me to first get the book distributed to the educational market, and Nina Linebaugh and others at Teacher's Discovery for their enthusiastic support for my books. Special thanks go to Ian Croxall of warflag.com for permission to use some of his beautifully- drawn flags in this book. Thanks also go to Rob Raeside, Director of Flags of the World at http://flagspot.net/flags/ for use of the Russian Imperial flag. Finally, I would like to thank the students of Yerba Buena High School in San Jose, California and Henry M. Gunn High School in Palo Alto, California for play-testing these games. Without their patient suggestions for improvements and clarifications this book would not have been possible.

Table of Contents

1. Roman Emperor Simulation — 4
2. Medieval Conversation — 12
3. Christopher Columbus Trial — 15
4. Martin Luther Trial — 32
5. French Revolution Simulation — 36
6. Taking Colonies: A World History Writing Assignment — 51
7. Great Powers Game (W.W.I) — 53
8. W.W.II Debates — 77
9. Cold War Simulation — 81
10. World History Counterfactuals: "What if...?" — 99

Simulation Title	National Standards Number	Description	Page Number
Roman Emperor Simulation	Era 3: 3A	Describe the political and social institutions of Rome	86
Medieval Conversation	Era 4: 4B	Change in the status of peasants & women	120
Columbus Trial	Era 6: 1A-C	Transoceanic interlinking of major regions of the world from 1450-1600	165
Martin Luther Trial	Era 6: 2B	Understanding of the Reformation	176
French Revolution Simulation	Era 7: 1A	How the French Revolution changed society	206
Taking Colonies	Era 7: 5B	Motives of Europeans in imperialist expansion	236
Great Powers Game	Era 7: 5B	Motives of Europeans in imperialist expansion	236
	Era 8: 2A	Causes of WWI	252
W.W.II Debates	Era 8: 4A	Causes & consequences of WWII	266
	4B	Scope and human costs of WWII	268
Cold War Simulation	Era 8: 5A	Global power shifts, how the Cold War developed, and competition of the USA & USSR for power and influence	270
World History Counterfactuals	All eras	"What if...?" questions covering all eras of World History	Entire book

Introduction

This book is an exciting collection of role-playing simulations for Social Studies classrooms. Although most of the simulations are written for World and US History, some of them would work equally as well in Economics or Government classes. All of these simulations have been play tested in classes ranging from Junior High to High School and at ability levels ranging from sheltered classes to honors.

What is a role-playing simulation?

Role-playing simulations attempt to put the student in the position of a person in a particular time and place. Most of the simulations involve group problem solving and conflict resolution. The students are given a character sheet which describes the groups needs and desires, a brief description of the historical problem and a copy of the rules of the game. Familiarity with fantasy role playing games is a plus, but certainly not required. The individual assumes the role they choose and makes decisions as the character would make during that particular time period. No pre-set limits are placed on a particular person's choices as long as they are within the realm of what was historically possible. Because of the freedom to choose in these games the outcome is very unpredictable. No two classes finish the simulation in the exact same way which leads to some very interesting classroom discussions about why things turned out the way they did, what could have happened differently, and how the simulation compares to what actually occurred in history.

How are these activities different from other simulations?

Unlike many simulations that are commercially available, these games can usually be played in one or two class periods. Their open-ended nature allows for playing up to one week if time permits, but after a couple of days you will find that most of the possibilities have been exhausted and continued play will have only limited instructional value. Another key advantage to this system is the cost. Everything you need to play these simulations can be reproduced out of this book. There are no tiresome charts to deal with and minimal set up and cleanup time required allowing for maximum role-playing time. As much as possible, pieces have been kept to a minimum to make cleanup and storage easier and to keep costs down for teachers on a budget. The emphasis is on role-playing so that the student can get as much as possible out of their personal learning experience and not get tied up in the mechanics of a complicated rules system.

How are the simulations used?

The best way to use these simulations is at the beginning of a unit when students have little prior knowledge of the historical outcome of a particular conflict. This allows a clean slate for actions instead of a predictable imitation of history just because "That's the way it had to be". When the teacher does begin the regular instructional part of the unit, the students will automatically make comments like, "Wow! That is just like what happened in the game" or "Now I understand why they did what they did". We all know that students remember better what they do than what they heard or read about, so these simulations allow for an unforgettable experience, which will bring history alive for them.

After the simulation is completed the teacher can lead a very interesting discussion of why things happened the way they did and how they might have turned out differently in the game or actually did turn out differently in other countries. This debriefing period is the most valuable portion of the activity. Students will be eager to participate because they were active stakeholders in the decisions made instead of passive listeners hearing about other people's problems from long ago. The activities build historical understanding, empathy for the viewpoints of others and group decision-making skills.

Follow up activities might include an essay comparing the game to what actually occurred in history or a visit to the internet newsgroup on alternative history where the students' questions can be bounced off a group of history professors, students and aficionados across the world. This can be a very valuable form of feed back. The simulations can also be used at the end of a unit for a form of alternative assessment to see how well they can apply the skills they have learned to an actual historical problem.

What do students have to say about these simulations?

Invariably students rate these activities among their favorite activities of the year. Returning students have stated that they are the things they best remember about the class years later. Under motivated students will often flourish in these activities because they have found a place were their abilities can shine. Gifted students enjoy the challenge of adding as much realism and detail to the activity as possible and often enjoy taking a leadership role in the bargaining.

Many students have commented to me that "This is the first time I have ever been interested in a history class" or "This makes me feel like I was really there because it was so exciting". Often discussion over what has occurred will pour over into other classes, lunchtime or after school. Students will compare what happened to their friends' classes and eagerly return the next day to see if the outcome is as they expected.

How did this book come to be?

The author has played role-playing games since he was a teenager himself. The fun and unpredictability of the outcome of a given situation got him thinking about how history might have been different. As a lover of history and a player of every kind of game from checkers to fantasy role-playing and historical miniature battles it was a natural step from tinkering with rules to developing his own games. He has experimented with these games from his first year of teaching, improving upon them every year based upon feedback from students. As he began to share these simulations with colleagues, they unanimously urged him to publish them to make them available for other teachers.

Roman Emperor Simulation Teacher's Guide

Objective: This simulation is a fun and lively way to teach the chaotic way in which the Romans decided accession to power.

Duration: 1-2 class periods.

Materials: A copy of the rules for each student and a copy of the social group description for each member of the group. A fake laurel wreath and white robe or toga add a little theatrical value to the simulation.

Procedure:
1. Choose 2 students to be rival emperors and 2 students to be their co-emperor assistants.
2. Divide up the rest of the class into the four social groups. Hand out a copy of the rules to everyone and a copy of the social group description to each member of the group.
3. Conduct negotiating and wars according to the rules on the student handout.
4. Stop the simulation and conduct debriefing.

Teacher Recommendations:
1. The students who run for emperor and co-emperor need not be male for the sake of the game because a few of the emperors' mothers or wives seemed to be the real power behind the throne regardless of who held the title. Make up a suitably phony Roman name that everyone can have fun with. Roman names always had three parts like Ricardus Dominus Jacobus.
2. Try not to lead the students too much as to what they should demand from the emperors or what to do with an emperor they don't like. Let them be creative and explore the options for themselves.
3. Remind the social groups that they cannot ask for something that didn't exist in Roman times like guns, electricity or equal rights for women.
4. If an emperor is crowned ham it up and give a laurel wreath and have everyone say "Hail Caesar!" loudly three times. If he is assassinated, act it out and have the student immediately return to his seat. This may shock students when they find out how easy it is to get rid of somebody, but explain to them that this was common in Roman times and go on with the game. After a while a strong emperor will emerge or the situation will degenerate into anarchy. Stop the simulation and proceed to the debriefing.
5. If any candidate or social group declares a rebellion or civil war, simply take a fresh count of actual armies pledged to each candidate at that moment and write the totals on the board. Eliminate an

equal number from each side until one or the other candidate prevails. In the event of a tie, the Empire goes into a chaotic year of interregnum until the crisis can be resolved. In other words, start a new turn by going through the negotiations and voting phases again. N.B. If a social group withholds its armies from both candidates for emperor, it is possible for them to raise an independent army and fight against one or more candidates or other social groups. If they are victorious, they appoint one of their own as emperor and deal with the losers in any way that they wish.

Debriefing:
1. How orderly was the transfer of power from one emperor to the next? How easy was it to get power? How easy was it to hold onto it?

2. Why did the Romans use such a crazy system to choose their leaders? Was it only because of their pledge to never live under a hereditary monarch who could become a tyrant? Why didn't they just stay with the government of the Republic?

3. How would these power struggles affect the stability of the Empire? Do you think they contributed to its fall? Do you think Rome would have lasted longer if they had come up with a better system for succession?

4. How is our government like that of Rome and how is it different?

Roman Emperor Simulation

Object of the Game: To choose an emperor and co-emperor who will become the undisputed rulers of Rome.

Players: Two teams of opposing candidates for emperor. The emperor is aided by a co-emperor who helps him come to power and will replace him if anything should happen to the emperor.

The Social groups: There are four social groups who listen to what the emperor promises them and pledge their money and armies to support one of the factions or the other. The four groups are The Roman Army, The Senators, The Provincial Leaders, and The Barbarians. These groups are from 2-8 people chosen randomly from the rest of the class.

How the game is played:

1. **The negotiation phase:** During this phase the emperor and his co-emperor make their way around to each group generously promising to give each group whatever they want. They listen carefully to each group's demands and promise to do what they can when they become the emperors. Each emperor has 10,000 soldiers and 10,000 talents (Roman money) to do with as he pleases each turn. He may also promise patronage for the arts, building projects, circuses, roads, protection, and special trade privileges in order to get votes. Once chosen as supreme ruler and living god, he will probably do what he wants however. He may also deal with those who vote against him in any way he chooses.

2. **Vote count:** Put each emperor and co-emperor's name on the board and record the armies and talents pledged to each. If anyone has a majority of the money he becomes the emperor, if not a civil war breaks out. In the case of a war the armies from each side eliminate each other until there is a victor. The victor is crowned emperor, proclaims himself a living god, and issues his decrees. In

case of a tie or deadlock a new round of negotiating and vote counting takes place until it is broken.

3. **Consolidating power:** Once the decrees are pronounced each social group is then asked if they will accept the new emperor. If everyone agrees then a reign of peace begins. The talents pledged to a candidate are, in effect, taxes collected and paid to the candidate to allow him to form and conduct his government. If one candidate has the majority of the money (his own or that pledged by the social groups) he has a vote of confidence and carries out the government until overthrown. The money is spent each turn and must be raised again each turn of the game. Note that the social groups do not have any independent source of wealth of their own. Their only money is that which was previously given to them by the emperor candidates. By giving some or all of it back to a candidate they are showing their support for him. If any one social group does not acknowledge the new emperor, then they may choose to not pledge their money the next year. They may also raise new armies, start a civil war with their own army, proclaim one of their own as emperor, or attack the person of the emperor himself. Unlike talents, armies raised each turn may be added to those from previous turns to increase the total size of an emperor's or social groups' forces. Once an army is pledged to an emperor, they are under his exclusive control and can be used in any manner he wishes.

4. **Death of an Emperor:** Should the emperor lose, he is dead and his co-emperor is the new emperor. The new emperor must re-negotiate to see if his rule will be accepted and so on. Anyone who proclaims himself emperor must first gain support, beat all of his challengers, and then set up a new government in his turn. Each year (one game turn) the emperor may issue new decrees and then try to stay in power till the next year. Any emperor who can stay in power five years wins the game.

The Roman Army

You are a rough and rowdy bunch, which has seen many wars and is not easily persuaded to join a cause. You come from many parts of the Empire and know of its riches, but you also know that they are not yours. You will follow a man with reasonable charisma if he can promise you enough money and a chance for promotion. You will retire with land of your own and Roman citizenship after 40 years of service, but you would probably fight much harder for someone who can promise you these things immediately after his victory in the civil war. Choose carefully; after all why throw away a sure thing of lifetime duty with a great retirement on some upstart who may only drag you down with him if he falls? If he isn't a good soldier you have little respect for him. On the other hand, if he dies, you can always try and appoint one of your own as Caesar; it has worked on occasion in the past.

The Senators:

You are a crafty bunch who knows well the ways of persuading men to follow you. You have made a career of exchanging privileges for your clients' votes: this is what got you in the Senate in the first place. The Senate as a whole already controls several provinces, but would like to control more. You are, as a rule, suspicious of Imperial power, and make long speeches about returning to the glorious days of the Roman Republic when the Senate and consuls alone ruled Rome. You are also highly suspicious of the power of the Army because of its role in the downfall of the Republic. Most Emperors rise out of the Senate however, so you are not too idealistic to take an office under an emperor to advance your own chances for the slot someday. You could also stand to make a lot of money if you squeeze the province for all its worth. You are already a major landholder and quite wealthy, but you are not above bribes.

The Provincial Leaders:

You have got enough problems to worry about at home. Why follow a new leader from Rome who may only get you in trouble with your superiors in Rome? He had better promise your province a better status than it has now or you will just stay neutral in the civil war. You are making out just fine taxing your province to death, and selling privileges to local officials. You are under pressure from your citizens, however, to lower taxes, improve the roads and aqueducts, and get a nicer theater, coliseum and baths. Food would also be nice to have to help protect against famine. Most of all, your citizens are sick of being treated like second class people, they want full Roman citizenship to enjoy the privileges of Roman Law. You would also like some troops or protective treaties to protect your merchants from thieves and pirates, put down rebellions or repel those nasty barbarians who keep sneaking over the border.

The Barbarians:

You are great admirers of Roman culture, food, money, beauty, etc. You have been staring across this border for a long time and covet your neighbors' goods. It would be tempting to try and cross that border for some harmless sacking and pillaging, but you know by the way that your ancestors were treated that the Romans get pretty vengeful about that sort of thing. For the time being, it is much safer to do it the legal way and ask the Romans for some money, land, or help in fighting your rival barbarians. In exchange you could provide troops to join the Roman Army, get civilized and do what they are told for a change. (Who knows? You might even learn some of their secrets to use against them some day when you get the chance.) You might also threaten to join the other side at a really embarrassing moment if you don't get your way; this has proved to be a ready source of cash in the past. The thing that you want more than anything, however, is to become Roman citizens-this is the stuff that fantasies are made of and you know that you are last in line for it.

Medieval Conversation Teacher's Guide

Objective: The students will try to think in the Medieval mindset to appreciate how different modern times are. It will stimulate good critical thinking and discussion as well as being fun.

Duration: 1 class period.

Materials: A copy of the Medieval Conversation handout for everyone.

Procedure: Though not a simulation in the strictest sense, this activity is best done in pairs so that the students can bounce their ideas off of each other. Hand out a copy of the Medieval Conversation handout to each student. Have the students discuss the words and phrases and circle or underline those which would have been unknown or not used in the Middle Ages.

Teacher Recommendations: To answer a common student question: "No, you can't just circle every word!"

Debriefing:
Go over the list and explain which things were not in existence in the Middle Ages. This includes inventions, unknown places or figures of speech. This will lead to a very lively discussion of just what was known at that time. Do some research on etymology for words like "okay" and "good-bye" for example. Foods can lead to a good discussion of Medieval trade routes and which things were later introduced from the Arabs or America.

Answer key for the Medieval Conversation.
Most of this will be obvious to you, the teacher, but a lot of it will be new to your students. Can you catch anything else not listed below?

1. "Hello" is, of course, modern. Some etymologists think it was originally "hail to you".
2. The title "Mr." wouldn't have been used- perhaps Master or Squire.
3. Weekends didn't exist until American labor unions acquired that right in this century.
4. "OK" is an American phrase of debated origins.
5. Surfing was invented in Hawaii, a place unknown to Medieval Europe.
6. Cars and highways are, of course, modern inventions.
7. Restaurants grew out of the courts of Renaissance princes whose feasts grew so elaborate that multiple servants and menus became necessary. It wasn't until travel increased in the Renaissance that inns began to offer anything close to what we think of as a modern restaurant.

8. "Terrific" once meant literally "inspiring terror", and would not have been used in a positive sense.
9. "You bet," a bit of American gambling slang, wasn't used until the 1800's.
10. Dieting was virtually unknown until the health movement of the 19th century grew out of increased medical knowledge.
11. Cola is made from cola nuts, which originated in Africa. The drink didn't come along until 1887.
12. Vegetarianism derives mostly from certain types of Hinduism. Most Europeans had no contact with India.
13. Modern pizza would have been impossible without the pepper and the tomato, both from the New World.
14. Hamburgers are American from about 1912, and there would be no American cheese without an America!
15. Iced drinks go back to the Romans, but only as a luxury for the rich who could send a servant to a mountain for ice!
16. Tea, sugar, and lemons came from Asia.
17. Roller skating waitresses are from the 1950's in America.
18. Divorce was practically unheard of in the Middle Ages.
19. Nearly everyone was a Catholic in the Middle Ages. Martin Luther didn't come along until 1483.
20. "That's the pits" is American slang from the 1970's.
21. Cinnamon is from Asia.
22. Dollars are from the German "thaler" a crown coin minted since the Middle Ages. The American dollar was first minted in 1787.
23. The cash register is also a modern invention-1879.
24. The radio was invented in 1906.
25. Some say rap began in the 1960's in New York City. Various other dates and places are also claimed.
26. The San Francisco 49'ers are named for the men of the California Gold Rush of 1849. American football was developed in the 1880's.
27. Manned flight in various forms began as early as the 1700's.
28. Sigmund Freud, the famed psychiatrist, began his publishing career circa 1900.
29. Ciao is an Italian word that didn't make its way into American slang until Italian films became popular in the 1950's.
30. Patronymic names such as Jones came from "son of John" and occupational names such as Smith first developed in the Middle Ages, but the combination of first and last names in the present form didn't become common until overseas traveling and printing developed in the Renaissance.
31. The truncating of phrases such as "See you later" began in the 1980's and continues with ever more clipped phrases being created in the foreseeable future.

Medieval Conversation

Directions: How many things can you find in this conversation that would be out of place if it were held in the Middle Ages? Discuss these words and phrases with a partner and circle or underline them below.

"Hello, Mr. Jones," said Mr. Smith, "How was your weekend?"
"Okay." replied Mr. Jones. "We went surfing in Santa Cruz."
"Oh, really!" said Mr. Smith, "How did you get there?"
"We drove our Minivan down Highway 17," Mr. Jones responded.
"Would you like to stop for a bite to eat?" questioned Mr. Smith entering the restaurant.
"Sounds terrific," agreed Mr. Jones as they entered together.
As they took a seat, the waitress asked, "May I take your order?"
"You bet," affirmed Mr. Jones, "I'd like a diet cola and a vegetarian pizza."
"I'd like a mushroom burger with American cheese and an iced tea with lemon and no sugar." added Mr. Smith.
"Thanks," quipped the waitress as she skated away with their order.
"How's things with your wife?" queried Mr. Smith.
"Not so good." replied Mr. Jones. "She wants a divorce".
"Oh, no!" said Mr. Smith, "Why?"
"Oh, she's a Protestant and I'm a Catholic," Mr. Jones answered.
"That's the pits," reflected Mr. Smith.
The waitress brought their bill and suggested, "Would you like a cinnamon roll for dessert?"
"No, thanks," they both said.
"That will be $10.87 please," stated the waitress.
"Do you accept credit cards?" asked Mr. Smith. "Sure." said the waitress, as she took their bill to the register.
Mr. Smith commented, "What's that song on the radio?"
"I don't know," replied Mr. Jones, "some new rap song about the 49'ers."
"Well, I gotta fly," said Mr. Smith.
"Me too," said Mr. Jones. "I've got an appointment with my psychiatrist about my first marriage."
"Ciao," said Mr. Smith. "Later," replied Mr. Jones.

Christopher Columbus Trial Teacher's Guide

Objective: To appreciate the controversies surrounding the life of Columbus and how they have affected his legacy to this day.
Duration: 2-3 class periods.
Materials: A copy of the depositions for each witness and his or her lawyer.

Procedure:
1. Choose a very brave volunteer (one with a dramatic flair if possible) to represent Columbus. You may wish to pick a gifted student to research Columbus in advance so that he can answer more elaborate questions.
2. Decide whether the judge will be played by a leading student or the teacher.
3. Divide the rest of the class into four groups:
Witnesses for the Prosecution
Witnesses for the Defense:
5 lawyers for the Prosecution
5 lawyers for the Defense
The jury (9-12 members)
4. Begin by having the person playing Columbus, the witnesses and their lawyers read their depositions and conduct further research (if necessary) to get more familiar with their character.
5. The Lawyers then draft a series of questions they will use with their witnesses.
6. The Lawyers then rehearse the questions they will use with their witnesses to prepare the manner in which the witnesses will answer the questions.
7. Conduct the trial with modern methods of questioning and cross-examination, but explain that the actual trials were quite different in those days. In the actual hearings, recorded as the *Pleitos Colombinos* (Columbian Lawsuits) by historians, Columbus himself was not actually on trial. His heirs were appealing to the Crown for a restoration of his rights, titles, and privileges, particularly that of Viceroy over all of the lands that he discovered and those adjoining them with their accompanying revenues. Countersuits were filed by the Pinzòn family and other witnesses who claimed that Columbus did not deserve credit for the discoveries. The proceedings dragged on for years to no one's satisfaction. Eventually, years after Columbus' death, his heirs were forced to agree to a settlement whereby they accepted title to a tiny portion of the vast lands discovered by Columbus, a small annuity and the right to use the title Admiral of the Indies and other minor titles. For more information, see the article about the *Pleitos* in the bibliography below.
8. After questions have been asked about all of the charges by both the prosecution and the defense the jury can ask for any points of clarification and then meets privately to vote on whether Columbus should be convicted separately on each charge or not. They may then suggest an appropriate punishment such as stripping him of his titles, rewards etc. Note that Columbus may only be sentenced to death if the charge of treason is proved.

Teacher Recommendations:
1. Keep the objections to a minimum as it ruins the authenticity and flow of the trial.

2. To add more realism, you as the teacher can play the role of the King of Spain (even though he might not have been present) and conduct the trial in the manner of guilty until proven innocent, as was the way of monarchs in those days. You can show very obvious bias and a will to convict. This will surprise students, but tell them, "We are the King, and we can do whatever we want."

3. Remind your students that this trial never actually took place. Some of these people could not possibly been present at the time of the trial. The depositions that follow are merely based on what they have said in their writings or what others have said about them. They are not direct quotations. They are approximate summaries of their views based on the closest reading of the historical sources possible. It was necessary to paraphrase their words in order to make them more easily understandable to the modern reader and to have a concise document for the purposes of this simulation. The author has tried to be as faithful to their original ideas as possible. For further research, consult the bibliography below.

4. Remind the jury that they represent the Council of The Indies, a group of nobles appointed by the king to administer the colonies and supervise their exploration and development. Their primary interest is to see that law, order and prosperity are restored to the colonies as quickly as possible. (In the actual proceedings, they were decidedly biased against the heirs of Columbus and dragged out the settlement as long as possible, hoping that the parties would give up. In the meantime they were free to give the titles and income from the colonies to whomever they wished).

5. You will notice that the charges of Columbus being a genocidal maniac or the sole founder of the slave trade in the Americas are conspicuously absent from this simulation. That is because they are based on rather poor modern scholarship that deliberately ignores any historical source that had anything positive to say about Columbus. Just as past generations glossed over the faults of Columbus in order to build a cult of hero-worship around him, some scholars today refuse to see any admirable traits in the man to further their political agenda. It is important to teach students that most historical figures had good and bad behaviors and characteristics and that to oversimplify them as all good or all bad is simply not being a good historian. It is not fair to single-handedly blame Columbus for all the sins of the explorers and conquistadors, nor is it accurate to portray him as a flawless hero or saint.

Debriefing:
1. What did you learn about Columbus that you did not know before?
2. In the actual trial of Columbus only the witnesses against Columbus were allowed to speak and modern methods of cross-examination and rules of evidence were not used. Why do you suppose that this was done? How did it affect the outcome of the trial and Columbus' fortunes?
3. How has the legacy and image of Columbus changed over time and why?
4. Why is it that the negative impression of Columbus dominates most treatments of Columbus these days? Are these accounts truly fair and unbiased?
5. If the judge ran the court in a more traditional fashion, use these questions: What surprised you about the way this trial was conducted? What words would you use to describe it? Unfair? Fixed? Kangaroo Court? Why do you suppose the king acted this way? How was this different from a modern court?

Bibliography:

First and foremost, the author would like to recommend one of his other books because of its general treatment of all the explorers mentioned in this simulation:

Di Giacomo, Richard. *The Influence of Renaissance Humanism On The Explorers of The Italian Era of Discovery.* San Jose, California: Magnifico Publications, 1991.

For the actual lawsuits filed for and against Columbus see:

Phillips, William D. "The Testimony of Empire: The Columbian Lawsuits" Terrae Incognitae 32 (2000).

Other helpful works for background research:

1. Arciniegas, German. *Amerigo and the New World: The Life and Times of Amerigo Vespucci.* Translated by Harriet De Onis. New York: Alfred A. Knopf, 1955.

2. Crosby, Alfred W. Jr. *The Columbian Exchange.* Westport, Co.: Greenwood Press, 1972.

3. Colón, Hernando (Ferdinand Columbus). *The Life of the Admiral Christopher Columbus.* Translated by Benjamin Keen. New Brunswick, New Jersey: Rutgers University Press, 1959.

4. de Las Casas, Bartolomé. *History of the Indies.* Translated and edited by Andreé Collard. New York: Harper & Row, 1971.

5. Markham, Clements R. trans., notes, and intro. *The Letters of Amerigo Vespucci and Other Documents Illustrative of His Career.* New York: Burt Franklin, reprint ed., n. d. Originally published by Hakluyt Society.

6. Morison, Samuel E. *Admiral of the Ocean Sea: A Life of Christopher Columbus.* Boston: Little, Brown and Company, 1942.

7. Morison, Samuel E., trans. and ed. *Journals and Other Documents on the Life of Christopher Columbus.* New York: The Heritage Press, 1963.

8. Pohl, Frederick J., *Amerigo Vespucci: Pilot Major.* New York: Colombia University Press, 1944.

9. Williamson, James A. *The Cabot Voyages and Bristol Discovery under Henry VII.* Cartography of the voyages by R. A. Skelton. Glasgow: Robert Mac Lehose & Co. Ltd. The University of Cambridge Press for the Hakluyt Society, 1962.

10. Williamson, James A. *The Voyages of the Cabots and the Discovery of North America.* London: Argonaut Press, 1929.

Christopher Columbus Trial Simulation

The charges against him:
1. Breach of contract-he didn't discover the Indies; therefore the King and Queen don't owe him a peso
2. Mismanagement of Hispaniola. He was a terrible governor.
3. Misappropriation of the reward for the first sighting of land. He stole the money from others who sited land first.
4. Impersonating a lord of noble blood. He was not a noble so he should not be allowed to be a viceroy of the Indies for the King and Queen.
5. Conspiracy to commit treason against Their Most Catholic Majesties, the King and Queen of Spain. He has defrauded them and conspired with our enemies.

Characters:
Christopher Columbus, known to the Spanish as Cristobal Colon and in his native Genoa as Cristofero Colombo
The Judge (the teacher or a leading student)
5 lawyers for the Prosecution
5 lawyers for the Defense
The jury (9-12 members) representing the Council of the Indies
Witnesses for the Prosecution:
1. Francisco de Bobadilla, royal representative to the Indies
2. Martìn Alonso Pinzòn, captain of the Pinta
3. Gonzalo Fernàndez de Oviedo, chronicler of the History of the Indies
4. Master Rodrigo, Former Archdeacon of Reina, Spanish Theologian
5. Guatauba, a Taino Indian
Witnesses for the Defense:
1. Ferdinand Columbus, son of the Admiral of the Ocean Sea
2. Giovanni Caboto (John Cabot), fellow explorer
3. Bartolome' de Las Casas, defender of the Indians
4. Paolo Toscanelli, professor of mathematics, geography, and philosophy
5. Amerigo Vespucci, fellow explorer, head of the Royal academy for Exploration of the Indies

Witness for the Prosecution #1
Deposition of Francisco de Bobadilla, royal representative to the Indies

Cristobal Colon (Columbus) was a cruel and corrupt governor of Hispaniola who, through false claims and mismanagement, ruined the colony, oppressed its Christian and Indian inhabitants, and plotted to wrest control of the colony for his own possession or to hand it over to the control of our enemies. He overtaxed the Indians, and forced the Spaniards to do hard labor for him and go for long periods without pay. He falsely accused innocent people and punished them harshly. He was unable to fairly collect the taxes due from the Indians to the Sovereigns. He was unable to control their uprisings. When unable to deliver the gold and riches that he said this colony would produce for Spain, he enslaved some of the very same Indians he told everyone earlier to not to harm. Not that I am against slavery itself, for, as everyone knows, the Indians enslaved each other before we arrived. I happen to feel that the cannibals among them deserve it for their devilish practices, but why enslave those who are loyal to us? He was a very poor judge of which Indians were loyal and which were not. Innocent ones were killed and treacherous ones were pardoned. Many lives were needlessly lost.

He is cruel and greedy and deserved to be replaced. Had he remained the Governor the colony surely would have fallen into ruin. I was sent as a most humble servant of Their Most Catholic Majesties to report on the status of the colony and the uprising. I regret to have to say that Christopher Columbus and his brother are totally incompetent and that I had no choice but to assume the leadership of the colony for myself to restore some sense of order to the chaos they have created. After listening to the grievances of many upstanding citizens who were harmed by them, I strongly feel that no one who bears the name Columbus should ever rule these lands again. I agree with our Most Catholic Majesties that Spanish lands should remain in Spanish hands from now on.

Witness for the Prosecution #2
Deposition of Martìn Alonso Pinzòn, captain of the Pinta
1492

Colon (Columbus) was a fraud. It is I who found the lands of the Indies first for the glory of Their Majesties. I returned to Spain first to stake my rightful claim. His poor leadership often led the men to the brink of mutiny. He made judgment errors in the course of navigation that could have cost us our lives. He recklessly endangered us to further his own ambitions. He defrauded humble sailors of their rightful prize from the King and the Queen for being the first one to sight land. On this account, I seek nothing for myself, but only that the simple sailor who first sited land be given the prize money for himself. As if Colon needs the money after all of the vast funds and rewards lavished upon him already! Why cheat a poor sailor of the 10, 000 maravedis annuity when that money could mean a lifetime of security to a poor man like Pedro Yzquierdo and nothing more to Colon? He is a traitorous foreigner who lorded it over loyal Spanish patriots who were humbly serving their righteous sovereigns. He is not to be trusted and should not be paid anything since all of the important work was done by others.

I am the one that arranged for all of the important introductions that made this journey possible when everyone else said it was foolishness and could not be done. I lent him money and provided him with ships. Columbus could have never found the Indies without my help. I was the first one to sight land in the Indies, the first to land in Hispaniola, and the first one to return to Spain. I was the one to encourage the men to go on when they all wanted to turn back. I was even the one to give Columbus the idea to sail westward. I told him of a letter I saw in Rome wherein the wise King Solomon told of a rich land named Cipangu that could be reached by sailing west from Spain. It is only fair that I, a native-born Spaniard, be given half of the treasure that I have brought to the King and Queen of Spain. I once called Columbus my friend, but that filthy, lying foreigner has defrauded me of what he promised and all that I worked so hard to gain. My only hope is that as I lay dying, God will see fit to bring justice to my heirs and restore the riches and honor that are due to my family.

Witness for the Prosecution #3
Deposition of Gonzalo Fernàndez de Oviedo

    I am the author of the great work *Historia General y Natural de las Indias* (General and Natural History of the Indies) the first comprehensive work to chronicle the history of the region from its earliest times under the rule of our great sovereigns, the King and Queen of Spain. I know this land, Columbus and his deeds better than few other men alive. While Columbus had some admirable traits, he has made some inexcusable errors that cast shadows of doubt upon his ability to rule these colonies, and even upon whether he truly deserves to be called their discoverer. Most of all, he is far from the first person to consider finding new lands to the west. Did not the great philosopher Aristotle mention the land of Atlantis as being to the west of the straits of Gibraltar? If such an authority as Aristotle says that the Carthaginians had already been there and people are now being sent to the Inquisition for questioning the word of the most wise Aristotle, then what are we to say of Columbus' claims that he got their first?

    A commonly repeated story these days is that Columbus first thought of sailing westward when he saw the Indies clearly marked on a map made by a Portuguese man Vicente Dias, who had already been there. This man had been blown off course by a storm and had seen these islands, but had been unable to find them on several return ships. Is it not at least possible that Dias, or some other Portuguese Andalusian or Basque navigator, put this idea into Columbus' head? No one can prove this is true, and I am not really sure I believe it myself, but, if it is true, then all claims he has made as to revealing the Indies to the rest of the World and all of the titles and revenues that come with it are falsely gained. This would make Columbus no more than an imposter and a usurper. As to the claims of the Pinzòn's, they are great navigators, but I think that it would have been shameful for them to mutiny against their commander, and they clearly did not. I will leave it up to this court to decide who deserves the proper credit for discovering these new lands and returning to Spain first. I want no further part of these proceedings.

Witness for the Prosecution #4
Deposition of Master Rodrigo, Former Archdeacon of Reina, Spanish Theologian

When Columbus came to us he was a poor tradesman who only pretended to be a scholar. Columbus' ideas were based on faulty knowledge of geography and history. He dared to add his own changes to the long-accepted maps of the great Greek geographer, Ptolemy. He deliberately underestimated the circumference of the globe to make his proposal sound more feasible. He misinterpreted the Scriptures when he said that the world is 2/3 water. Many great philosophers disagreed with him. Even though Their Most Catholic Majesties were busy with the righteous crusade of driving the Moorish infidels from our land, Columbus kept harassing them until they gave in and let him try his Enterprise of the Indies. He proved nothing by going there, however, because others went to the Indies before him. There have been Spanish colonies in the Indies for as far back as the Carthaginians. Even the Portuguese went there before Columbus did. He probably got the idea from them.

Columbus did nothing new, so the King and Queen owe him nothing. He is foreign born and had a Portuguese wife. For all we know he could be a spy for our enemies! Columbus said that he would pledge all of the money he gained from his conquests to start a new crusade. Well, I haven't seen any new crusades started lately. Besides, he has been to the Indies four times, and still hasn't found the wealth mentioned by Marco Polo. Despite all of this, he has the nerve to demand to be made the king of the new lands he found and be given a large share of its wealth for him and his heirs forever. Even a fool with only a basic understanding of the law knows that if you don't deliver upon your part of the bargain in a contract, you can't expect any reward in return! Who does he think he is? We have put up with this fool for long enough. Give him some pittance of a settlement and give the proper credit and reward to loyal Spaniards like the Pinzòn's who have served God an their country faithfully in these troubling times.

Witness for the Prosecution #5
Deposition of Guatauba, a Taino Indian

When I first met Columbus I thought the gods had come to our island. He and his men looked so strange to us, but he seemed warm and friendly. He seemed genuinely interested in learning our ways and offered us interesting items like bells and mirrors, which we had never seen before. I still remember the first time I saw my own face in a mirror; I must have jumped back three or four steps in amazement! Because I learned their language faster than the others, he asked me to accompany him as a translator.

At first it was interesting, but I soon longed for home. Columbus could be very kind at times, like the time he rescued my tribe from a group of cannibals that was planning to eat us, but other times he grew very obsessive and greedy. At every new island we went to he would ask the same questions, "Have you seen Cathay, Cipangu, the Great Khan, the cities of gold?" It got be pretty comical after a while as I kept translating the same message back to him that the other Indians said, "Oh, the gold, that's way over there on that other island." Amazingly, Columbus never caught on that the Indians didn't know what he was talking about and were just trying to get rid of him.

One day Columbus said that he was going to take us back to his country to prove to his chief that we had been to "The Indies", wherever that is. After crossing more water than I had ever seen, we still hadn't arrived at his island. I panicked and jumped overboard. Though I hated to leave Columbus because he had always been kind to me, I had to get back home. Luckily some friends picked me up in their canoe. I eventually returned home several years later. I heard later that some of my friends were not so lucky. They drowned or died of diseases shortly after arriving in Spain.

To my horror and amazement my home island was nothing like what I had left. Everyone was dying from these horrible little red dots all over their skin. They all had a high fever and a terrible thirst. Many are falling every day now. Most of my friends and family are already gone. As if that is not bad enough we were tricked into being made slaves by the Spanish and made to work long hours growing crops for them or mining until we collapse with exhaustion. Columbus has now ordered that we take those beautiful little bells that he gave us (how I love their sound) and fill them with gold once a month. Doesn't he know that it is impossible?! When my friends complained to him that there wasn't enough gold on the island to do that, he had them killed! Now, I hate the man. I don't know what happened to the man I once called my friend. I believe in this new god that Columbus brought with him, maybe He will call out one of the Spanish to show them the error of their ways. May God forgive Columbus, for I cannot.

Witness for the Defense # 1
Deposition of Ferdinand Columbus, son of the Admiral of the Ocean Sea

I know what you are thinking, "How can a man's own son give an impartial account of him?" Well, I am more than just a dutiful son. Although I know him like no other and am proud of his great deeds and accomplishments, I am also his chief biographer, curator of his collection of maps, charts, and writings, a humanist scholar, historian and navigator myself. I have collected books from many parts of Europe. I have served on a royal commission that corrected marine charts, commissioned pilots, and decided the rival claims of Spain and Portugal over the Moluccas. What's more I accompanied the great Admiral on one of his voyages and saw his great strength of command and divinely guided decision making first hand.

Oviedo is a poor scholar who knows no Latin and relies on others to translate documents for him. He has read things into Aristotle's writings that were not there, misinterpreted documents and deliberately misled people. Who is he to take away credit for deeds done by men much greater than him? God led my father to the Indies to fulfill a heavenly mission to reach those living in spiritual darkness. How can Oviedo cast doubt on this and give the credit to others based on rumor alone? What kind of historian is that?

Oviedo claims that the Carthaginians or other ancients came to the Indies first, but he offers no conclusive proof that these lands were west of the Straits of Gibraltar. If they were large lands with great forests and navigable rivers, how could this be possible on islands, no matter how big? Surely there was a mistake in his translation of Aristotle. If these lands were so great, why didn't the ancients stay there and their existence remain common knowledge? He also says that a few years before Columbus, Portuguese explorers were accidentally blown westward and found the Indies. How is that possible when the winds blow from west to east not from east to west? That would be an even bigger miracle than the ones my father witnessed as God led his way through the Enterprise of the Indies.

Most of the other accounts of Columbus are written by men who did not know him. Their books are full of errors, either from ignorance or from malice, because they wish to give credit for Columbus' discoveries to others so that they could gain something for themselves. I have carefully exposed each one of their falsehoods in my book *The Life of the Admiral Christopher Columbus* at length, so I will not trouble you with them now. Who can know a father better than his own son? What could I possibly gain from lying about him? There are those like Agostino Giustiniani who would insult my father's heritage, claiming that he was not of noble origins. Even if he is not, which is more important a man with a noble title who does nothing important or a common man who does noble deeds? My father was not a simple tradesman. He studied at the University of Pavia and was well versed in letters, geography, history and philosophy. He was an expert mapmaker, always updating his maps with details from interviews with

Deposition of Ferdinand Columbus (continued)

well-traveled sailors. He prepared well for his journeys by scouring every book he could find written since ancient times that mentioned the Orient.

He traveled to the limits of the known world and interviewed anyone he could find that had been near the Indies. He was a navigator without equal. He prepared for his trips by studying all the winds and currents before he departed in order to be sure of a safe return. He traveled through treacherous waters filled with dangers never before seen such as hurricanes, coral reefs, and deadly areas with no wind at all where many lesser men would have perished. To those who would say that he was cruel, greedy or incompetent, I say that nothing could be further from the truth. He was a pious, humble man who suffered great persecutions at the hands of others. First, they doubted him, then they mocked him, and then, when they found out that he was right all along, tried to rob him of his due rewards. Bobadilla is a corrupt man who sided with the leaders of the rebellion against the rightful ruler of the colonies, Columbus, the duly appointed Viceroy. He stole the Crown's properties and enriched himself at their expense. He nearly drove the colony to ruin by his mismanagement. The Pinzòn's are traitors who only wish to steal from Columbus what they could not accomplish on their own. Their insubordination to Columbus' commands was testified to by many witnesses. They nearly ruined the first expedition several times by disobeying orders and disappearing off in a direction of their own or failing to report back to the Admiral at the appointed time. They should be punished for their disloyalty and open rebellion against the Viceroy because it is the same as rebellion against the King and Queen. In contrast, Columbus' motives were only to bring greater glory to God and to Spain. His loyalty was proved again and again by his many years of faithful service to the Crown. He should by all rights be named a saint and one of the greatest figures in history for the untold thousands he has led to the light of salvation.

Witness for the Defense #2
Deposition of Giovanni Caboto, fellow explorer

You probably know me best by my English name John Cabot. My son Sebastiano (Sebastian) and I have been engaged lately in trying to find a shorter route to the Indies than Columbus did. I admit that I owe a great deal to my friend Columbus. We not only share the same land of our birth, but the fate of being rejected by other Italians and having to explore instead for strangers. For it was his knowledge of the use of the new invention called the globe which was instrumental in convincing King Henry that it was indeed easier to reach the Indies from a higher latitude such as England than one closer to the equator, such as Spain. I felt badly that England had turned Columbus down earlier, but I was able to persuade the King to give the voyage a try under my leadership. He gave me a few ships, and was cautiously optimistic. Well, he was so overjoyed at my successful return that he gave me many more ships with which to confirm that I had indeed reached China, and to claim its wealth and return it to England. [Editor's note: since this deposition was recorded it should be noted that Master Cabot never returned from his second voyage and his entire expedition vanished without a trace].

He has even discussed allowing my son to explore an eastward route to the Indies by traveling over Russia. It has come to my attention that some disreputable people are now doubting Columbus' abilities and claims. I cannot understand this. I have never met a finer mapmaker or navigator than Columbus. He was truly an inspiration to me. I found him to be a fine scholar and a gentleman of keen wit and great knowledge. What's more, I have seen the Indies in exactly the place where he predicted they would be. I can't wait to get back to them to convert the heathens and bring glory and riches to my adopted country that has treated me so well. Although I explore for a different country, I do not consider myself a rival of Columbus as some do. As we learned when studying the writings of Marco Polo and others together, there are plenty of riches for everyone! First come, first served!

I do not try to denigrate his claims nor doubt his accomplishments as others do for their personal gain. If Columbus says something is true, then it is. He is a great and learned man. I hear that the king of Spain is talking about establishing an academy for navigators with Columbus at its head. What better man to lead it than the very man who inspired an entire generation of explorers to find the quickest route to Asia and to explore every unknown corner of any new lands which we may find? It is my most cherished dream that I, or my son Sebastian, may some day join, or even lead, this great academy. If the King of Spain puts this much trust in Columbus, then surely he is worthy of all the honors, titles and royalties that have been granted to him.

Witness for the Defense #3
Deposition of Bartolome' de Las Casas, defender of the Indians

I was once a conquistador. I once brutally misused the Indians for my own selfish gain. I witnessed others torture, humiliate, and even mock the Indians for their child-like trust and naiveté while all the while laughing at the ease of their ill-gotten gain. Finally, when I could take no more, I was able, through the Grace of God, to see the error of my ways. I underwent a heartfelt conversion and I have pledged the rest of my life to serve these most humble of God's creation, the Indians. I agree with Columbus who said in his journal, "They are a friendly and well-dispositioned people...I want the natives to develop a friendly attitude toward us because I know that they are a people who can be made free and converted to our Holy Faith more by love than by force...I think they can easily be made Christians." It is a tragedy that others did not follow in the example of this godly and upright man. Instead they disobeyed his orders and ran rampant throughout the land. They deceived the Indians, stole their treasures and land, raped, mutilated and murdered them. Then they had the audacity to tell the Indians that God had meant for them to be our slaves because they have no souls.

Well, I could not sit still for this. I have outlined their atrocities in great detail in my book, *Historia de las Indias* (History of the Indies). I have debated the greatest theologians in the Spanish Empire and proved to them that Indians do indeed have souls, and that they should be treated as our brothers not as animals. I have denounced those would go against my godly friend, Columbus, and trick the Indians into submitting to slavery by the ruse of having them agree to a Latin pronouncement that they cannot understand. This is an outrage! Columbus begged the righteous Queen to outlaw this practice, and when he began to round up violators of her royal decree, they had him bound in chains and returned to Spain as a common criminal! Surely, this is a great injustice.

Instead of being grateful to Columbus for his great deeds and benign leadership, they have tried to permanently bar him and his family from governing the very lands that he discovered. He has made them wealthy and their greed has blinded them into calling him a fraud and stripping Columbus of all his titles authority and wealth. May God have mercy on their souls for perpetuating such an insult to one of the greatest men of our age. One who is so humble and mild that he never even utters a curse word and who prefers to spend his time with clergymen. Dare I say that I have seen him live a life holier than many of my fellow members of the clergy? Perhaps he should be made a saint when he dies.

Witness for the Defense #4.
Deposition of Paolo Toscanelli, professor of mathematics, geography, and philosophy

[Editor's note: Toscanelli died in 1482, so he never lived to see Columbus set sail for America].

You may be surprised to hear me say it, but Columbus was not the first one to suggest that sailing west to reach the Indies might be a shorter route than the easterly route taken by the Portuguese. It was my idea actually, and I freely admit that he copied the idea from me. I even sent him a map showing routes for the journey and the distance that must be crossed. You may also be surprised to learn that Columbus admits this himself. You see, he was not the first one conceive the idea, he just became the best advocate for it. I am a man of letters. I write works on philosophy, mathematics, geography and many other subjects. I realized that in Columbus I had found a kindred spirit. He was a well-learned man who readily absorbed my ideas. We corresponded regularly as he grew increasingly excited about the prospect of reaching the Indies faster than the current Portuguese route.

What set Columbus apart was that he was a man of learning _and_ of action. Alas, I am too old to follow my dreams. I can do no more than speculate as a scholar. I am, what you might call, an armchair explorer, like the great ancient writer Ptolemy who speculated a route around Africa without actually trying it. I pointed out to Columbus the riches mentioned in the East by Marco Polo and others. I told him and his potential sponsors that there had already been Christian missions requested by the Great Khan and that they would be very receptive to Christianity. As Hieronymus Muntzer has pointed out, Aristotle also said that the distance between East and West was not great and that there are similar plants and animals on both sides. If the Vikings could find Greenland, and the Portuguese the Azores, why can't Columbus cross from our lands to those of the East?

That young man Columbus impressed me as the kind of man with the determination to actually make my dream a reality. He is doggedly pursuing the crowns of Europe with the idea of the enterprise of the Indies until, some day soon, an equally daring sovereign will decide to give it a try. He will convince the doubters and skeptics who said it couldn't be done. People doubted that men could live in the torrid heat of the tropics until the Portuguese went there and proved it. Columbus shows great courage and leadership. Because he knows so many languages he could keep a multi-national crew united facing many great dangers until they reach their goal. The whole world will soon reap the benefits of his daring and determination. He is worthy of all of the honors and rewards that are due to him.

Witness for the Defense #5
Deposition of Amerigo Vespucci, fellow explorer, head of the Royal academy for Exploration of the Indies

I currently hold the job which was originally designed for Columbus, that of training other explorers. I have sailed for both Portugal and Spain and have fought against the limitations of small-thinking men who cannot see beyond their perceptions of the lands that they are exploring. They have preconceived notions of what they will find and which routes are best, even when the evidence right in front of them contradicts these notions. When I encountered such men I openly broke with them and pursued what I knew was the right course regardless of the risk to my safety or reputation. Because of this I have found many new lands not even mentioned by Marco Polo or the Ancients. I have met Columbus and shared many ideas with him. He is the greatest navigator of our time. His bravery and tireless work ethic have inspired us all. His only limitation is that he stubbornly insists that he has found Asia, and keeps asking for permission to return to the lands that he explored to confirm it even though he is now old and failing in health. After repeated denials, I heard that he is currently begging the King to let his son go and finish his quest. What I came to realize through my own explorations is that Columbus is wasting his time. He will never find proof that he reached Asia because he is still far from those lands.

I now believe that the lands that I explored to the south of Columbus' voyages are not among those mentioned by Polo at all, but a *Novus Mundus*, or New World. This is because I have seen rivers that were much too large to exist on mere islands. In all my extensive journeys I never once saw any of the cities or peoples mentioned by Polo or the Ancients. I still believe that Asia is obtainable by sailing westward, but that this can only be done by going around the lands I found to the south. I hope to return to the place where I was forced to turn back on my last voyage and find a passage or strait that would allow me to go beyond this land and continue to Asia. I wish that Columbus shared my views, but he insists that he has already reached Asia and only needs a bit more proof to convince his critics. He thinks that the lands that I found were the Garden of Eden or some other previously hidden region, not a New World.

There are those who say that I have claimed credit for discovering the New World and that I am an imposter and usurper who is trying to steal the glory from Columbus. Unscrupulous publishers are adding things to my written accounts of my voyages that I never said, but I am powerless to stop them. They are selling altered versions of my account without my permission. These men are liars and thieves. They care more for exciting fiction and profit than the truth. Some have even proposed naming the New World after me because they have never heard of Columbus or do not believe him. I want no part of this. I deeply respect Columbus and, despite our differences, am eternally indebted to him for his influence and inspiration for my own voyages of discovery. We have both been victims of men who would exploit our names or discredit us for their own personal gain.

Martin Luther Trial Teacher's Guide

Objective: This simulation is a very useful way to teach the difference between the beliefs of Protestants and Catholics, the beginning of the Reformation and the life of Martin Luther.

Duration: 1-2 class periods.

Materials: Give a copy of the beliefs chart to each student to be turned in and graded at the end of the period.

Procedure:

1. Begin by having the students complete the chart comparing Catholic and Protestant beliefs in small groups of 2-3. Try to mix the groups so that a variety of religious beliefs are held by its members. Any mixture of Protestants, Catholics, or non-Christians is okay as long as the group is not entirely comprised of either Catholics or Protestants. Sometimes the students will need a little help remembering which group they fit in, but ask them to tell you the name of the church or a few questions about their beliefs and you can usually figure it out. The students then interview each other based on their prior knowledge of the subject.

2. Give them about 10 minutes to work on the chart together. After they have filled out the chart with as many answers as they can, tell them the remaining answers. They can correct or add to their chart as necessary. Once every one has completed his chart the simulation can begin.

3. Choose a very brave volunteer (one with a dramatic flair if possible) to represent Martin Luther. Tell him that he will be asked a series of yes or no questions that he will always answer "yes". If you wish to have more authenticity pick a gifted student to research Martin Luther in advance so that he can answer more elaborate questions.

4. Divide the rest of the class into three groups: the Protestant panel, the Catholic panel, and the jury. The two panels will devise a series of yes or no questions based on each on the beliefs on the chart. Choose people and questions at random from the group to make sure that everyone understands the material and grade on participation. The Protestants should try to craft "softball" questions designed to make Luther look good or "get off easy". The Catholic group should design tough questions that

will try and trap Luther into making heretical statements. Sample questions are like these: "Do you believe that the Bible should be read in the everyday languages of the people?" or "Is it true that you married a nun?"

5. After questions have been asked about all of the issues by both panels the jury can ask for any points of clarification and then meets privately to vote on whether Luther should be convicted as a heretic or not.
(I have yet to see a no vote, but the students don't know that in advance).

Teacher Recommendations:
1. While completing the chart make sure that you stress that we are not debating who is right or wrong, we are just learning from each other. Don't let anyone feel uncomfortable because they are not a Christian. Just tell them that can be any group and that this is a way to learn about religions just like all of the other ones that we have studied in this class. Sometimes students will say, "I'm not a Catholic, I'm a Christian." Point out to them that everyone who believes in Christ is a Christian and that telling someone that they are not a Christian is a quick way to offend them. Also point out that this chart reflects the views of The Roman Catholic Church at the time of Martin Luther, and that some of these views have been changed in the years that followed.

2. To add more realism, you as the teacher can play the role of the Holy Roman Emperor at the Diet of Worms and conduct the trial in the manner of guilty until proven innocent, as was the way of monarchs in those days. You can show very obvious bias and a will to convict. This will surprise students, but tell them, "We are the King, we can do whatever we want."

Debriefing:

1. What surprised you about the way this trial was conducted? What words would you use to describe it? Unfair? Fixed? Kangaroo Court? Why do you suppose the king acted this way? How was this different from a modern court?

2. What did you learn about the beliefs of Protestants and Catholics that you didn't know before? What do they have in common? What is different about their beliefs? How have their beliefs changed over the years?

3. Why do you think that these differences sometimes led to conflict and wars between the two groups? Are there any countries where Protestants and Catholics are still fighting today? Do you feel that the two groups are more tolerant of each other in the USA? Why or why not?

Beliefs	Protestants	Catholics
The role of the Pope		
Praying to Mary		
Language of the Bible		
Who is a saint?		
The use of statues or icons		
Confession of sins		
Marriage of priests		
Salvation by Faith		
Age of baptism		
Method of baptism		
Sale of indulgences		

The French Revolution Simulation
Teacher's Guide

Objective: This simulation is a great way to get across the complexities of the party politics of the French and other revolutions in a clear and easy way. The results are extremely varied because the resulting constitution can be everything from a restoration of the monarchy to a modern pluralistic democracy and everything in between. This lays a very strong framework for the remaining portions of the World or European History course because all of the options discussed in the simulation for government were tried at some time or place or another between 1789 and today. It also begins to stimulate students' thoughts about the roots of dictatorship and totalitarianism in the Twentieth Century because some of the disturbing practices of a one party system such as banishing or killing their enemies were learned from this period.

Duration: 1-2 class periods.

Materials: Pass out a copy of the rules of the game to everyone, and a copy of each group's role to the members of that group. All constitutions should be drafted on a separate piece of paper and then read to the class as a whole to be voted upon.

Procedure:
1. Divide the students into 8 equal groups. Each group will carefully read its group description sheet to determine what the goals and desires are for each group. This description sheet will also tell each team whom its likely allies and enemies are. Each team will then discuss amongst themselves how they will go about gaining the support of as many social groups as possible.

2. Each team goes out and negotiates with each of the social groups. The team drafts a constitution explaining their new form of government.

3. Each social group listens carefully to the constitution and then decides which team will get their points.

4. Groups then modify their constitutions, solicit votes, or resort to violence to gain and keep power until a dominant or stable government emerges.

Teacher Recommendations:

1. Try to let the students be as open-ended in their possibilities for a constitution as they wish, but make sure they do not include anachronisms which would not have been considered in the 18th century like modern tax schemes, huge bureaucracies, or contemporary civil rights controversies. Blank forms for drafting a constitution can be duplicated from page 32 of this book. Voting can be done by writing the names of the four parties on the board and then having each social group state how many votes, armies, taxes and armies they will pledge to each party. You may also make a transparency out of page 33 of this book for keeping score each round. The social groups may hold some or all of these in reserve to use in another turn but must keep records to prove it. The winner is the party with the most votes in the first round. In the case of a deadlock the king stays in power and a new round of negotiating and voting takes place. This goes on until someone breaks the deadlock with a victory or an act of violence.

2. The teams, which represent the four parties, can promise whatever they want during the negotiations phase, but once they are in power they are not bound to do all that they promised. If they break a lot of promises and begin to behave tyrannically then ask those who are currently the outsiders what they will do to seek revenge and change the government more to their liking.

3. At first the game usually progresses in a friendly manner as the groups try to make a mutually agreeable constitution, but the party in power soon finds it impossible to please everyone or abuses its power and then divisions and sometimes conflicts result.

4. If the social groups or parties feel that they cannot live with the current government then ask them how do they wish to change it? Another round of voting? A deliberate act of violence or a general war? Try not to lead the students too much. Let them explore their options.

5. Should a war break out write the names of the four parties on the board and then tally up the armies pledged to each. Armies eliminate each other until a victor can be determined. In case of a tie, start the whole thing over with a new year of negotiating and raising support. If a social group likes none of the parties presented they may attempt to create a rogue army with one of their own as leader. This army may then attempt to defeat all others and establish their own government by force. You can even allow for foreign intervention by other monarchies or democracies if you wish. Pick a student to secretly represent a foreign power with 5 armies to contribute should he decide

to intervene. How long he wishes to retain his secrecy his entirely up to him.

6. Continue the simulation until there is a clear victor or hopeless deadlock. Parties will rise and fall, and many constitutions may be adopted and then later replaced. Ask the losing parties what they may have to compromise on in order to capture more votes or armies. If leaders are killed simply pick someone else in the group. Parties may merge with others or fade, but seldom die completely. Finally when you feel that all the worthwhile possibilities have been exhausted move to the debriefing phase of the simulation.

Debriefing:
1. Was there a clear winner in this game? Why or why not?

2. What role did the social groups play in making or breaking a party? Is it possible to make a government that they can all live with?

3. How did this simulation compare to the real French Revolution? How was it different?

4. What countries have come up with solutions similar to your own in their current or past forms of government? Are there governments today which fit the kinds of constitutions the four parties originally desired?

5. What other ways could the game have turned out? What else might you have tried? Do you think other governments have tried these options in the past or today? Is there anyone in current events that reminds you of the parties in this game?

6. How was the revolution like other world revolutions? How was it like modern dictatorships or monarchies?

The French Revolution Simulation

Time: circa 1789

Object of the game: to become the sole party in control of France and draft a constitution that will make the majority of people happy.

The teams:
The Radicals   The Liberals   The Moderates   The Royalists

Social Groups:
The Clergy   The Nobles   The Merchants   The Peasants

The teams (of 2-4 people each) will compete for the power, approval and wealth of the four social groups (of 2-4 people each).

How the game is played:
1. Each group will carefully read its group description sheet to determine what the goals and desires are for each group. This description sheet will also tell each team whom its likely allies and enemies are. Each team will then discuss amongst themselves how they will go about gaining the support of as many social groups as possible. Figure out what you will promise each group, but remember that you must try to do what you promised or lose their support later on.

2. Each team goes out and negotiates with each of the social groups. In exchange for the promises made to them each group can give away points to show their support for a team. The points are divided as follows:
10 points of taxes
10 points of military support
10 points of votes in the Estates General
10 points of party recruits

3. The members of the team report back to the team the results of the negotiations and the team drafts a constitution explaining their new form of government.

4. Each social group listens carefully to the constitution and then decides which team will get their points.

5. The winner is the team with the most points. Multiple rounds of the simulation can be played with each turn representing one year. Losing teams can try and gain additional support and overthrow the government. Whichever team is in control at the end of ten years is the winner.

6. The winner may deal with the losers in any way that they wish, but remember excessive violence only breeds resentment and retaliation among your enemies.

7. If at any time a team has exclusive control of the military they may proclaim their leader to be a dictator. If a dictator can stay in power for more than five years his team wins the game.

The Royalists:

You are people who profited from having a strong king in control. You miss the old days of absolute monarchy. France has had a king for 1,000 years, so why change now? What you would like is to get king Louis XVI or one of his relatives back on the throne. You like the old ways of Feudalism, central control, and deference to authority. You think that leaders should be born into a special class and that no one should lessen the power of the king. Your natural allies are the nobility and the clergy because they prospered under the old system and are afraid of what they might lose if something replaces it. You have limited support from some peasants who are loyal to their feudal lords and from some merchants who made money by selling and lending to the king.

The Moderates:

You are open to some change and reform but you don't want things to get carried away. You love the tradition and ceremony of having a king, but you would like him to under the control of a representative legislative body similar to the English parliament. You are against the excesses of absolute monarchy, but not against the idea of having a king itself. You simply want to limit his power to tax, make war and use terror, the army, and the courts to control his subjects. A good king can be the most efficient form of government and you would hate to see it replaced by forces you could not control. You have some following among rebellious nobles and clergymen who would like to be more independent from the king's control. Others may be happy to support you rather than see the monarchy replaced altogether for fear of what might follow it. The Merchants and the peasants will support you only if you include them in the representative assembly and introduce reforms such as lower taxes etc.

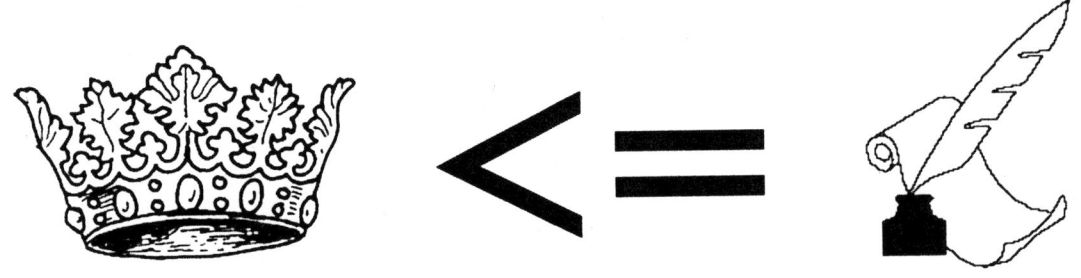

Written constitution

The Liberals:

You feel that the king is not really necessary anymore. If he continues to exist at all, it should only be as a figurehead. The real power of government should lie in the hands of the people through a representative legislative body with open discussion and voting. You believe that no one should have the right to take away your life, liberty or property and are prepared to protect them at all costs. You resent high taxes and want reforms in administration of government and the laws of business. You want to get rid of nobles and feudalism. You believe in capitalism and free trade. You believe in education and freedom to do whatever work one chooses to get ahead in this world. You do not feel that this power to vote and participate in government needs to be shared with the peasants because they have no property to defend and are not educated enough to know how to vote. You feel that the power of the Church should be under control of the government. You feel that its lands and money should be made available for average people to develop and gain a profit.

Written constitution

The Radicals:

You are fed up with the way things are and want immediate change. You think that the very idea of a king is wrong and all kings should be overthrown. You want the immediate vote for all citizens regardless of their property or birth. The real power of government should lie in the hands of the people through a representative legislative body with open discussion and voting. You believe in free access to education and opportunity for everyone. You hate the power of the Church and the nobles and believe that their property should be taken away and given to the peasants. You believe in religious toleration and complete separation of the powers of church and state. You might find support among the poorer merchants and the peasants if you could tear them away from the nobles. Both will insist that you include them in the representative assembly, lower taxes, and tax the nobles and the Church.

Majority rule!

The Nobility:

You like things the way they are, but you will support any arrangement that takes power away from the other social groups and leaves your lands, titles, and exemption from taxes intact. You resent the power of the king and the church, but do not wish to see them replaced entirely, as you wouldn't mind holding their jobs someday too. You don't trust the peasants because they are constantly running off of your lands and refusing to pay their feudal dues or complete their military service. You are used to leading the army and will be upset if anyone takes that away from you.

The Clergy:

You are conservative and do not like change of any kind. You feel that God places and removes kings at His will and that no one else should have the right to decide that. You are getting quite rich from the way things are and do not want to change. You compete with the nobles for power and influence, but would not like to see them replaced because many of your family members are in the nobility, and you need their protection. You like them just the way they are as long as they don't interfere with you. You are disappointed with the peasants because they are constantly running off of your lands and refusing to pay their feudal dues or service to the Church. You feel that it is not fair for you to pay taxes because you do God's work by taking care of the needy or underprivileged. You will resist all attempts to have your power or lands taken away because you feel that they belong to God and not you. Taking what is God's is a terrible sin. You don't like Merchants much because they sometimes cheat you and don't always pay their fair share of money in tithes to the Church.

The Merchants:

You have money and influence, but no real political power. You are fed up with the feudal system because you are not represented in the government. You like the money you get from the king, but feel that he tries to tax you and regulate your business too much. You feel envious of the power and influence of the nobles who only got what they have through birth. You worked hard for everything you have and no one is going to take it away from you. You have no great respect for the peasants because that is what you once were and would like to forget it. You want to share the power and influence of those higher up in society than yourselves. You respect the Church but are sometimes annoyed by their taxes and power.

The Peasants:

You have been at the bottom of the heap for a long, long time and want to get out. You deeply respect the king, the nobles, and the Church, but resent their abuses of power. You do all of the hard work, pay the major portion of the taxes, and have no representation in government. You think everyone else should be taxed and want the wealth, land and power of the other groups. You are jealous of the wealth and influence of the merchants and wish you could get out from under feudalism as well.

Outline for a French Revolution Constitution:

We, the _____ Party believe in the principles of:
_____
_____
_____
_____
_____

Under the new government, the following social groups will be allowed to vote: _____
_____
_____
_____

The role of the King will be: _____
_____
_____
_____
_____

The following taxes will be collected from the social groups:

Social group	Type	Amount
Peasants:		
Merchants:		
Clergy:		
Nobles:		

Land will be owned by: _____
_____

The role of the Church will be:
_____
_____
_____
_____
_____

The role of the nobles will be:
_____
_____
_____
_____

The following social groups will be allowed to serve in the army:
_____
_____
_____

Education will be available to: _____
and paid for by: _____

The French Revolution Simulation Vote Tally Sheet

Round # _____

	Royalists	Moderates	Liberals	Radicals
Taxes				
Military support				
Estates General Votes				
Party recruits				

Round # _____

	Royalists	Moderates	Liberals	Radicals
Taxes				
Military support				
Estates General Votes				
Party recruits				

Round # _____

	Royalists	Moderates	Liberals	Radicals
Taxes				
Military support				
Estates General Votes				
Party recruits				

Round # _____

	Royalists	Moderates	Liberals	Radicals
Taxes				
Military support				
Estates General Votes				
Party recruits				

Taking Colonies Teacher's Guide

Objective: This activity is done individually as a creative writing assignment, but it still carries the spirit of this book in the sense that the student must assume the role of another and write from their point of view.

Duration: 1 class period.

Materials: Hand out a copy of the Taking Colonies handout to everyone.

Procedure: Discuss with students what the backgrounds of some of the people listed below might be. Let them choose which person they will write about.

Teacher Recommendations:
1. Remind them to stay within the proper time period and avoid anachronisms.

2. Also point out that a person might have had mixed feelings about taking colonies. They might have liked it for some reasons and not liked it for others. They also might not have felt like taking colonies mattered to them one way or another.

3. Tell your students that most of all they should be honest and write as that person would have felt not as a modern person would feel.

Taking Colonies: A World History Writing Assignment

Description: The year is 1878. The Congress of Berlin has just finished and the scramble for colonies is on! Many countries do not yet have colonies or overseas possessions, possibly including yours. You hear a politician give a speech saying that it is time that your country join other great countries and take overseas lands to rule as their own. He says that this would bring your country wealth through new trade opportunities, new jobs, and a source for goods not found at home. He says that colonies would make us seem more powerful to other countries and give us the chance to civilize and Christianize the natives of distant lands.

Choose one of the people from the list below. Imagine that you are one of these people. How would they feel about taking colonies? How would it affect them? Would they have any special reason why they would think that colonies would benefit their country or them personally, or would they be against it? Perhaps they have mixed feelings or feel that it wouldn't make any difference to them personally. Use your imagination and write as they would think.

- A housewife from Paris, France
- King Leopold of Belgium
- U.S. ambassador to England
- A maid from London, England
- A farmer from Topeka, Kansas, USA
- A shipbuilder from Bremen, Germany
- A banker from Rome, Italy
- A naval captain from Bristol, England
- A sailor from Cadiz, Spain
- A fisherman from Lisbon, Portugal
- A rabbi from Warsaw, Poland
- A recent Italian immigrant to New York City, USA
- A sewing machine manufacturer from Berlin, Germany
- A Protestant minister from Amsterdam, The Netherlands

Great Powers Game Teacher's Guide

Objective: To understand the issues and challenges leading up to the First World War.

Duration: 2-3 class periods.

Materials: A copy of the rules for each student. At least one copy of the country description sheet for each group. A large number of cards in four colors representing the pieces for armies, navies, industries, and colonies.

Procedure:
1. Sides may be chosen in whatever way the teacher chooses, but it is usually better to give them out at random because not all countries start out even, just as it was in the real race for empire.

2. Go over the rules with the students.

3. Students read their country's description sheet and plan their strategy for diplomacy, economic, military, and territorial expansion.

4. Conduct negotiations.

5. Conduct wars and further negotiations as necessary.

6. Debrief.

Teacher Recommendations:
1. Encourage students to do the best they can even if they have a weak country. Weak countries can still win the game if the have the right allies. If the class is very large make up additional statistic sheets for small countries which remained officially neutral in W.W.I such as Mexico, Portugal, or Spain.

2. Use the pieces at the end of the rules to make the record keeping easier. Run them off in different colors and cut them up. Make a large amount of armies, navies and industries, but only one of each colony. Appoint students to sell and collect the pieces. Watch for cheating! It is very important to tell the alliances NOT to combine their stacks of pieces because all too often alliances fall apart and it is too hard to go back and figure out who had what at the beginning.

3. If a war is declared simply list the country on the board that started it and the country that is being attacked. Then ask who would like to declare for each side. Allow a few minutes to allow reluctant stragglers to commit or stay neutral and for some countries to change sides at the last minute if they wish. (This often happens in real wars). Once the numbers are tallied eliminate forces on both sides until there is clear victor. Armies cancel out other armies, and navies cancel out navies. The countries that started the war should always take the heaviest losses.

4. If all of the armies are gone, go to navies as a tiebreaker. Two navies equal one army when they land and convert to marines. If there is still no victor, go on to another round of negotiating and purchasing until another year of war is fought. Countries may change sides any time they want or drop out. You may even have multiple alliances going at each other at the same time. The only thing that matters is who is left the strongest when the fighting is over.

5. After the war is over the victors hold a peace conference and dictate the terms to the losers. These are up to the victors to decide, but they may include occupying or annexing the loser's home country, taking their colonies or a portion of their industry. If the losers stay unoccupied they may try to rebuild, make new alliances and seek revenge. Sometimes the victors may disagree on the fair share of the spoils and turn on each other in the next round of war. Continue the simulation until there is a clear victor or a hopeless stalemate and then move on to the debriefing.

Debriefing:
1. How did it feel to build your empire? How did the smaller countries feel about how it turned out? Which countries had the advantage at the beginning of the game? Why? How did your empire compare to the real one that your country actually gained?

2. In the long run what was more important to buy, armies, navies, industry or colonies? Why?

3. What did you do well? What do you wish you had done differently?

4. How successful were your alliances? Did they help you or hurt you? Could they be trusted? Why or why not?

5. If there were wars how did they compare to the real W.W.I? How would the world be different today if the war had turned out differently than it did?

Great Powers Game

Time: circa 1900

Players: Great powers of Europe, rising powers of Europe, America, and Asia, and lesser powers that wish they were great.

Goal: Make your country powerful by building industry, gaining colonies, building a strong army and navy and gaining strong allies. That way if a war breaks out you can win it.

How long the game is played: Each turn will represent one year. We will play until we reach 1920 or the Great War breaks out, whichever comes first.

How the game is played: Each player will represent one country. You will try to make your country as powerful as possible based on what you have to work with and your ability. Each country has a description sheet stating its strengths and weaknesses at the start. You will try to use the countries' income and your bargaining ability to gain further power and influence. Some countries are naturally bigger and richer at the start. This cannot be helped, so do the best that you can with what you have. Sometimes small countries do very well by growing and making the right friends.

You will continue to gain power, wealth, and influence until a war breaks out and then you must defend it. Try to make as many friends as possible so that you have allies if a war breaks out. Make written treaties whenever possible because people tend to "forget" what they promised. You can give, take, trade, or promise whatever you want and you don't have to tell anyone except the country you sign the treaty with. Remember how you treat people because "what goes around comes around", in other words if you always make threats or bully people around you may find yourself with very few friends when conflict breaks out. Remember, no matter how big you are, you can't take on everybody!

Spending your money: You may choose each year how to spend your money. Try to keep a balance. For example: don't spend so much on colonies that you have no army to defend them, or don't spend so much on the navy that you don't have any industry. Any money that you spend on industry or colonies stays in your economy each year, any money that you spend on the military is gone forever. In other words, if you buy a dollar's worth of industry or 1 colony your income goes up 1 dollar the next year. If you spend 1 dollar on the army or navy your income stays the same next year. So obviously, if you spend all your money on the military your country can never grow and everyone else will eventually pass you up.

Colonies: Whereas you can buy an unlimited amount of industry or military, there are a limited number of colonies to go around so try to get them early if you can. There are exactly 120 colonies available, not including the ones that you have at the start of the game. When the colonies are all gone you will have to fight with someone to take theirs away. Also be aware that certain countries have an interest in certain parts of the world and that taking a colony there will make that country upset with you. How you settle your disputes with other countries over colonies is up to you.

Wars: When 3 or more great powers are at war the war is called a Great War. All countries that have treaties with the existing countries fight it. War is done simply by counting up the forces of the groups of allies and declaring a winner. Note: a country can break a treaty and change sides or drop out of the war just before it takes place if they want to regardless of what they promised before. The forces in the war are recounted and then the war is fought. This is not a great way to gain friends and influence in the future however.

GREAT BRITAIN

Location: NW Europe
Size: small
Power: great
Friends: England has been an ally of just about every country in Europe at one time or another, but she prefers democracies over monarchies.
Enemies: England has been an enemy of just about every country in Europe at one time or another, but her most recent war was with Russia. It has been a long time since England has fought Spain, France or the U. S.. and she is hoping that those old hatreds are forgotten by now. There have been some disputes with France and Germany in recent years over colonies, but things seem to be getting better.
Goals: England's primary goal is to keep a balance of power in Europe. She does not want to let any one power dominate the continent. She has pledged to defend neutral countries like Belgium if any larger country tries to take them over. England will also try to defend free and unrestricted trade at all costs.
Strengths: England has the most powerful navy in the world, and everyone knows it. She also was one of the first countries to industrialize so she has a strong economy. England also has the biggest colonial empire in the world.
Weaknesses: England's many colonies require a huge army to keep them under her control. This leaves a very small army to defend England or to be used to attack other countries.
Income: 4 economic points per year.
Beginning Setup:
Army: 1
Navy: 3
Industry: 3
Colonies: 3

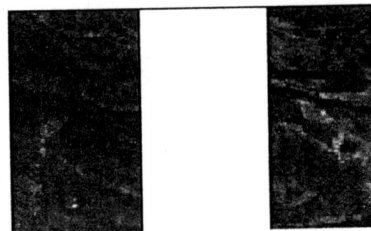

France

Location: W. Europe
Size: large
Power: great
Friends: France has no real allies, but has fought on the side of just about every country in Europe at one time or another when facing a common enemy. France prefers democracies over monarchies.
Enemies: All Europe remembers when Napoleon's armies tried to conquer the whole continent in the name of exporting France's democratic revolution and overthrowing kings and emperors. This has left most countries resentful of France because they did not like someone else telling them what kind of government to have. There have been some disputes with England in recent years over colonies, but things seem to be getting better. Germany and France fought a bitter war in 1870 in which Germany stole 2 of France's provinces. France has sworn revenge and says that some day Alsace and Lorraine will be taken back by force if necessary.
Goals: Defend France at all costs. Stop German expansion and reclaim lost lands. Expand colonial empire to rival that of England.
Strengths: Powerful army, which is feared and respected. Good navy. She also was one of the first countries to industrialize so she has a strong economy. France also has the second biggest colonial empire in the world.
Weaknesses: France's many colonies require a large army to keep them under her control. This leaves fewer forces to defend France or to be used to attack other countries.
Income: 3 economic points per year.
Beginning Setup:
Army: 2
Navy: 2
Industry: 2
Colonies: 2

Germany

Location: Central Europe
Size: large
Power: great
Friends: Germany has no real allies, but has a certain friendship with Austria because of the rulers being of Germanic ancestry. Germany's Kaiser is related to the King of England and the Czar of Russia. Germany prefers monarchies over democracies. Germany has a lot in common with Italy because both countries unified later than most of their neighbors; leading to fewer colonies and later indust-rial development.
Enemies: Most countries resent Germany's claims of superiority and threats to its neighbors. France, Denmark and Austria have lost territory to her in recent years There have been some disputes with England and France in recent years over colonies, but things seem to be getting better. Germany and France fought a bitter war in 1870 in which Germany stole 2 of France's provinces. France has sworn revenge and says that some day Alsace and Lorraine will be taken back by force if necessary. Russia is afraid of German expansion because the Germans have expressed an interest in taking Poland away from her because part of it was once German.
Goals: Attack weaker neighbors whenever possible. Prove to the world that Germany is great through quick, decisive use of new military power. Hold on to recent German territorial expansion and add new lands to it if possible. Expand colonial empire to rival that of England and France.
Strengths: Powerful army, which is feared and respected. Strong navy which rivals England for the first time ever. Rapid indust-rialization with a growing economy.
Weaknesses: Few colonies. Few allies. Army and navy are anxious to try their strength so they are not very patient or willing to compromise.
Income: 3 economic points per year.
Beginning Setup:
Army: 3
Navy: 3
Industry: 2
Colonies: 1

Italy

Location: Southern Europe
Size: medium
Power: great
Friends: Italy has no real allies, but has fought on the side of just about every country in Europe at one time or another when facing a common enemy or when it thought that joining the right side would help it gain power and influence. Italy generally prefers democracies over monarchies. Germany has a lot in common with Italy because both countries unified later than most of their neighbors; leading to fewer colonies and later industrial development.
Enemies: Most countries resent Italy's refusal to commit to long-term alliances as Italy has changed sides many times in the past. Italy hates Austria for controlling large parts of northern Italy before Italy's unification. Austria has lost territory to Italy in recent years, and the Italians still feel that some of the territory under Austria's control should rightfully be theirs. The same is true for Italy's relationship with France, but they do not hate the French as intensely. There have been some disputes with England and France in recent years over colonies, but things seem to be getting better.
Goals: Italy is jealous of its more powerful neighbors and wants to be like them. Italy will stay out of wars if possible to avoid being on the losing side and losing territory. Italy will join a war if they feel that other countries will reward them for their help. Italy wants to hold on to recent territorial expansion and add new lands to it if possible. Expand colonial empire to rival that of England and France.
Strengths: Average army and navy, which are yet to be proven. Gradual industrialization with a growing economy.
Weaknesses: Few colonies. No permanent allies.
Income: 2 economic points per year.
Beginning Setup:
Army: 2
Navy: 2
Industry: 1
Colonies: 1

Austro-Hungarian Empire

Location: Central Europe, Balkans
Size: large
Power: great
Friends: Austria has no real allies, but has a certain friendship with Germany because of the rulers being of Germanic ancestry. Austria prefers monarchies over democracies. Austria has a lot in common with Russia because both countries have conservative monarchies, which have joined to fight off the territorial expansion of Germany and France.
Enemies: Austria has lost territory in recent years to Italy and Germany as a result of their unification movements. As a result it has focused its attention on taking over small countries in the neighboring Balkan Peninsula. Austria faces a major challenge because Russia would like to expand into this area as well to gain access to warm-water seaports. The two countries have nearly fought each other in a major war many times by backing up the small country the other was trying to take over. Another enemy is the Ottoman Empire because many of the small countries Austria is trying to take over once belonged to the Turks and the Turks want them back.
Goals: Attack weaker neighbors whenever possible. Prove to the world that Austria is still great by gaining control of the Balkan Peninsula by standing up to Russia, Germany, Italy and the Ottoman Empire. Hold on to recent territorial expansion and add new lands to it if possible.
Strengths: Average army, which is still strongest in immediate area.
Weaknesses: The army is tied down by trying to keep many ethnic minorities within the empire from breaking away from the empire through revolution or foreign intervention on their behalf. Few colonies. Few allies. Many rivals. Small navy and a weak economy.
Income: 2 economic points per year.
Beginning Setup:
Army: 2
Navy: 1
Industry: 1
Colonies: 1

Russia

Location: Eastern Europe
Size: large   Power: great
Friends: Russia has no real allies, but has a certain friendship with Germany and England because Germany's Kaiser is related to the King of England and the Czar of Russia. Russia prefers monarchies over democracies. Russia has a lot in common with Austria because both countries have conservative monarchies, which have joined to fight off the territorial expansion of Germany and France.
Enemies: Russia is afraid of German expansion because the Germans have expressed an interest in taking Poland away from her because part of it was once German. Russia faces a major challenge from Austria because both countries are interested in taking over the Balkan Peninsula. The two countries have nearly fought each other in a major war many times by backing up the small country the other was trying to take over. Another enemy is the Ottoman Empire because many of the small countries Russia is trying to take over once belonged to the Turks and the Turks want them back. Russia also faces competition in Eastern Asia from Japan because both countries are interested in taking over parts of China. England has vowed to contain Russian expansion in Asia. As if this were not enough, revolutionaries at home are threatening to overthrow the Czar and form a democratic or communist government.
Goals: Russia would like to expand into the neighboring Balkan peninsula and take over small countries as well to gain access to warm-water seaports. Hold onto vast empire and avoid war whenever possible. Prove to the world that Russia is still great by gaining control of the Balkan Peninsula by standing up to Austria, Germany, England, Japan and the Ottoman Empire. Hold on to recent territorial expansion and add new lands to it if possible.
Strengths: Huge army, which is still feared and respected. Vast colonial empire.
Weaknesses: Army weakened by old-fashioned equipment and techniques and need to put down rebellions by colonies and revolutionaries. Small navy. Few allies. Many rivals. Small navy and weak economy.
Income: 3 economic points per year.
Beginning Setup:
Army: 3
Navy: 1
Industry: 1
Colonies: 2

Ottoman Empire

Location: Balkans, Western Asia
Size: large
Power: great
Friends: Turkey has no real allies, but has a certain friendship with France because they often have the same enemies. They also admire Germany's military power and share some of their enemies. Turkey prefers monarchies over democracies.
Enemies: Turkey has lost territory in recent years to Italy, France, England, Russia, and Austria, which it would like to reclaim. Turkey faces a major challenge because Russia would like to expand into its territory to gain access to warm-water seaports. The two countries have fought each other in small wars many times. Another enemy is Austria because many of the small countries Austria is trying to take over once belonged to the Turks who want them back.
Goals: Hold onto vast empire and avoid war whenever possible. Prove to the world that Turkey is still great by regaining control of the Balkan Peninsula and lost North African colonies. Standing up to the challenge from the other great powers to conquer the remaining Ottoman Empire and divide it amongst themselves. Hold on to what is left of your empire and add new lands to it if possible.
Strengths: Average army. Many colonies.
Weaknesses: Army is tied down in trying to keep more colonies from breaking away from you than already have. Few allies. Many rivals. Small navy and weak economy.
Income: 2 economic points per year.
Beginning Setup:
Army: 2
Navy: 1
Industry: 1
Colonies: 2

United States of America

Location: North America
Size: large
Power: great
Friends: U.S.A. has no real allies, but has a certain friendship with France and England because of democratic traditions and because they often have the same enemies. The U. S. strongly prefers democracies over monarchies.
Enemies: U.S.A. has no real enemies, but will fight against an enemy it feels is morally wrong. The U.S.A. has had some minor disputes with England, France, and Germany over colonies in South America and the South Pacific, but has avoided war every time.
Goals: Although America usually stays out of other countries' affairs, it is beginning to be interested in keeping a balance of power in Europe and Asia. She does not want to let any one power dominate either continent. America is eager to demonstrate new power and influence. America will also try to defend free and unrestricted trade. The U. S. is mostly interested in neutrality, but America will pick a fight with someone who tries to keep them from trading with either side in a war.
Strengths: Strong army and navy. Plentiful resources and rapid industrialization gave it a strong economy.
Weaknesses: Few allies. Reluctance to get involved in foreign affairs, especially wars.
Income: 4 economic points per year.
Beginning Setup:
Army: 2
Navy: 2
Industry: 3
Colonies: 1

Japan

Location: East Asia
Size: small
Power: small
Friends: Japan has no real allies, but has a certain friendship with England because they often have the same enemies. Japan usually prefers monarchies over democracies however.
Enemies: Japan is in direct competition with Russia for domination of the Chinese Province of Manchuria. They have almost gone to war over it several times. Japan has had some minor disputes with England, France, and Germany over colonies in China, but has avoided war every time.
Goals: Although Japan usually stays out of other countries' affairs, it is beginning to be interested in keeping a balance of power and establishing colonies in Asia. She does not want to let any one Western power dominate Asia. Japan would like to have Asia to itself, but is not yet strong enough to try and take it from the Western Powers. Japan is eager to demonstrate its new power and influence. Japan is mostly interested in neutrality, but will pick a fight with someone who tries to keep them from gaining colonies.
Strengths: Small army and navy. Rapid industrialization is giving it a growing economy.
Weaknesses: Few allies. Reluctance to get involved in foreign affairs, especially European wars.
Income: 2 economic points per year.
Beginning Setup:
Army: 1
Navy: 1
Industry: 1
Colonies: 1

67.

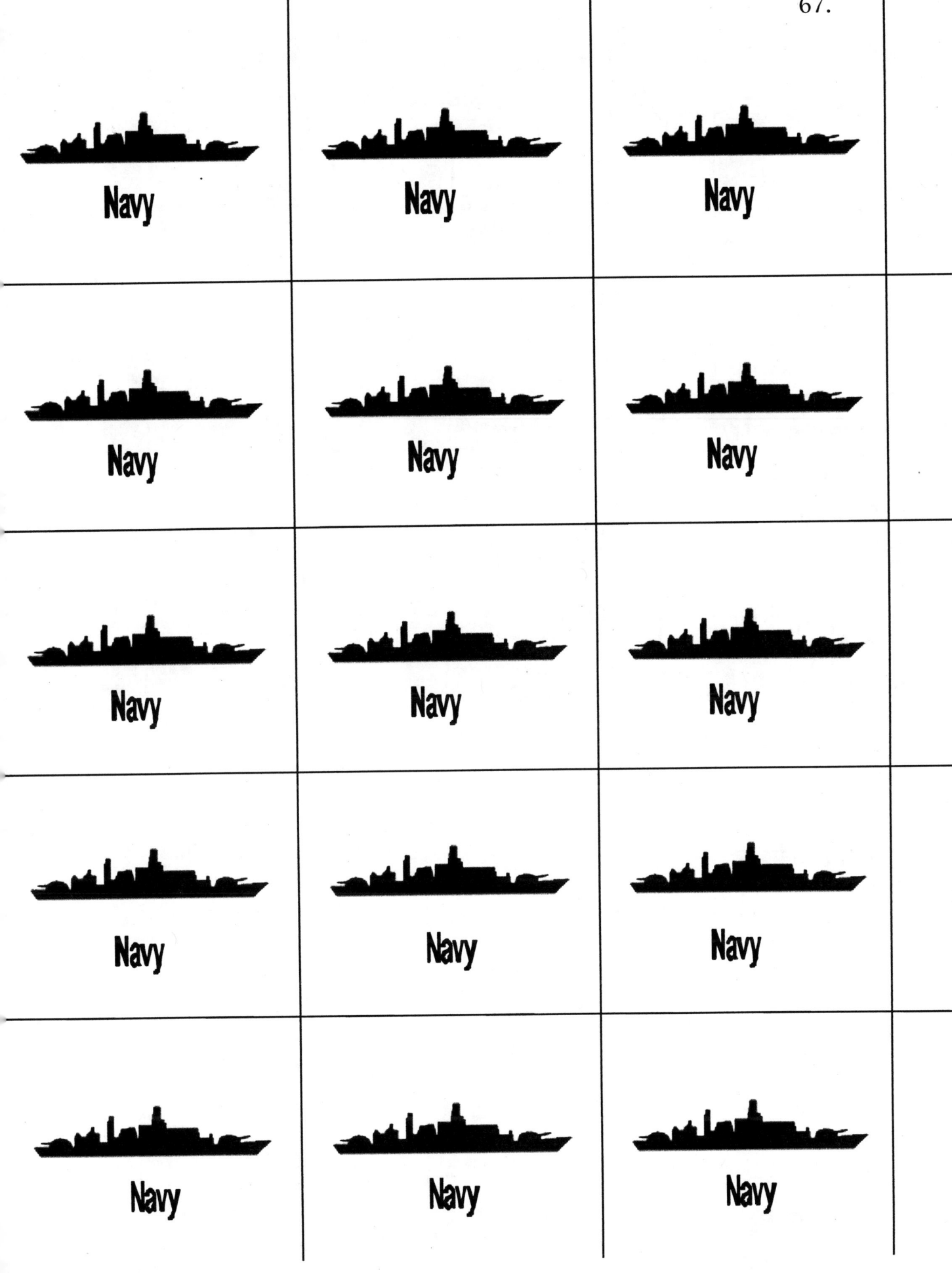

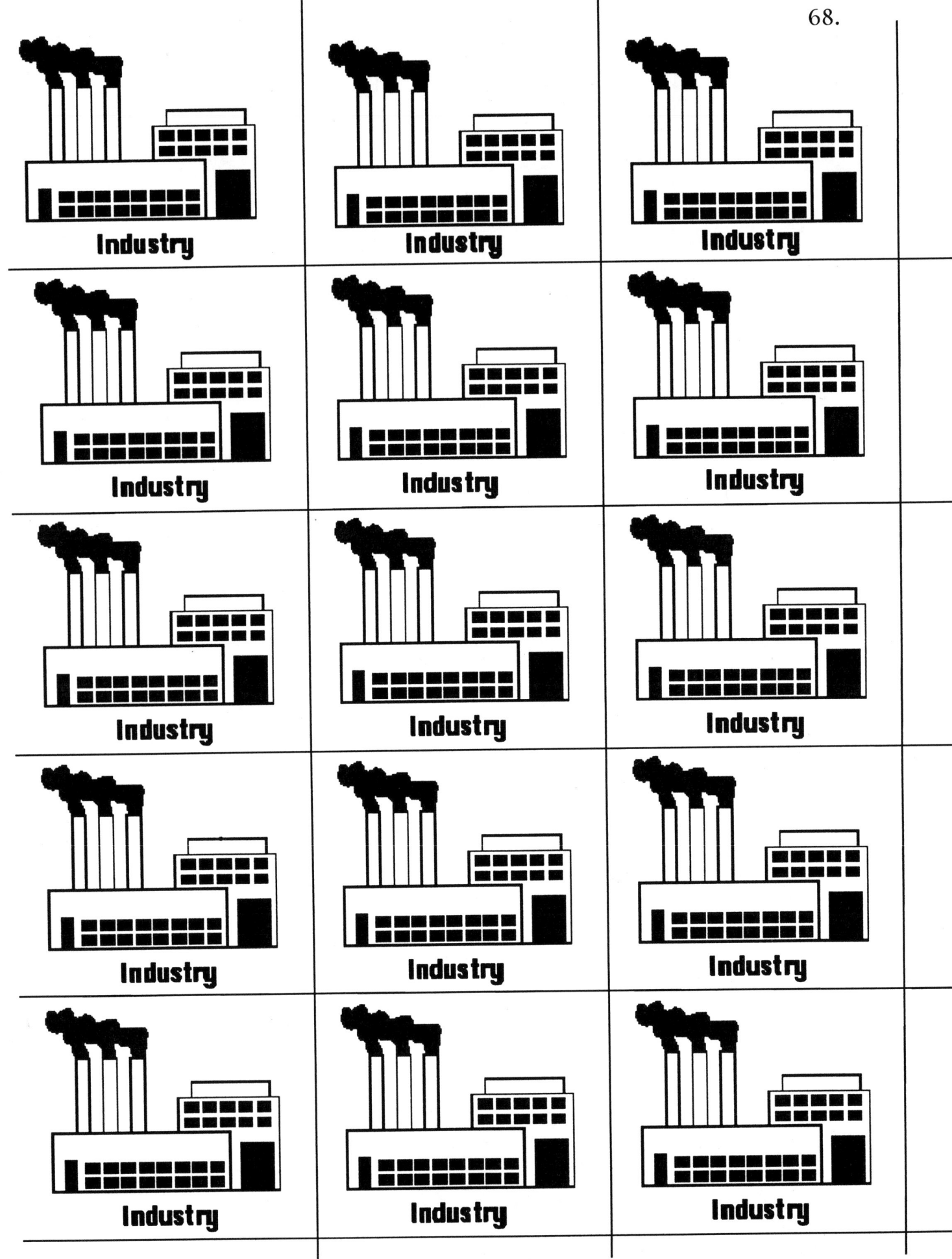

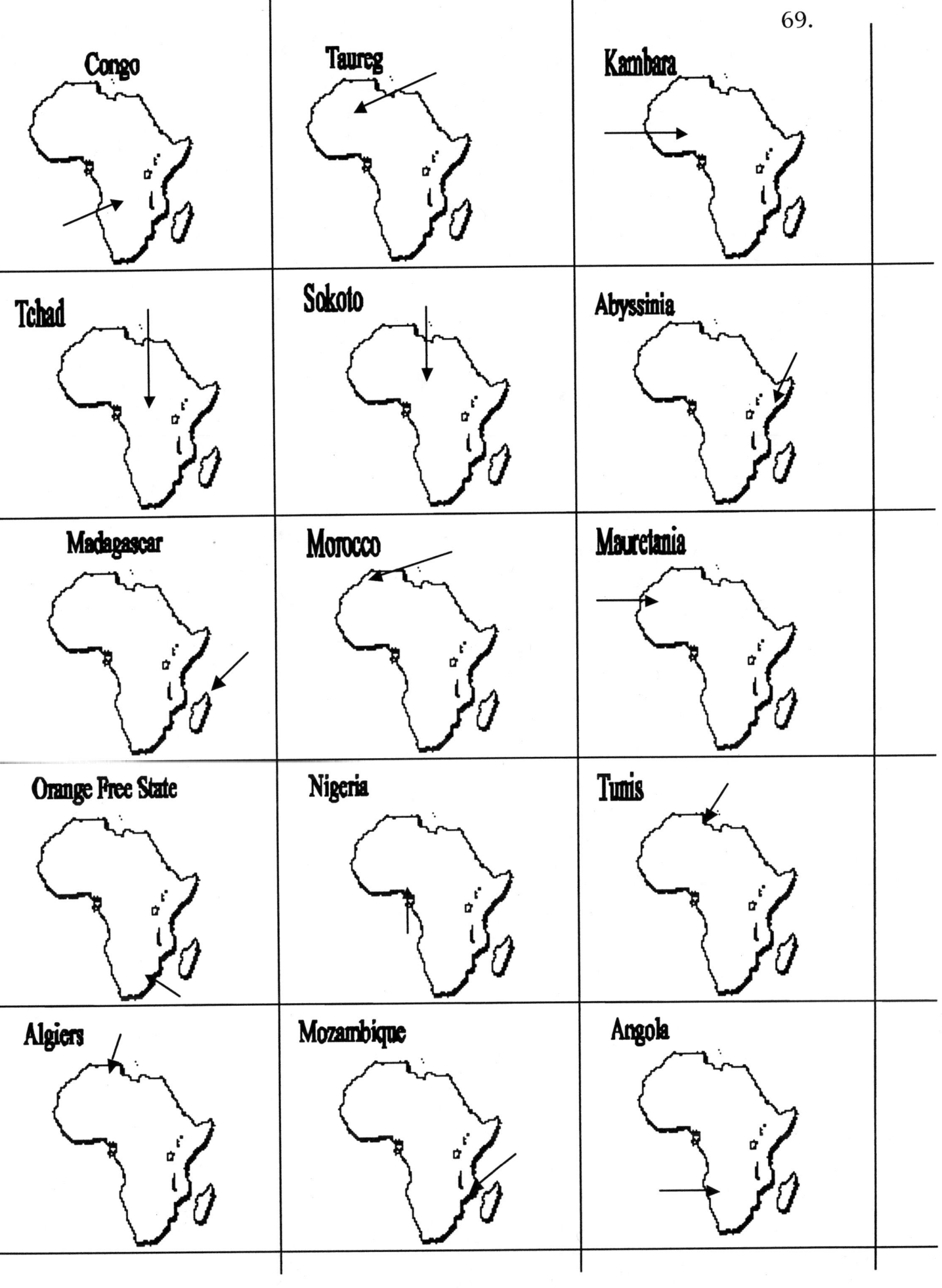

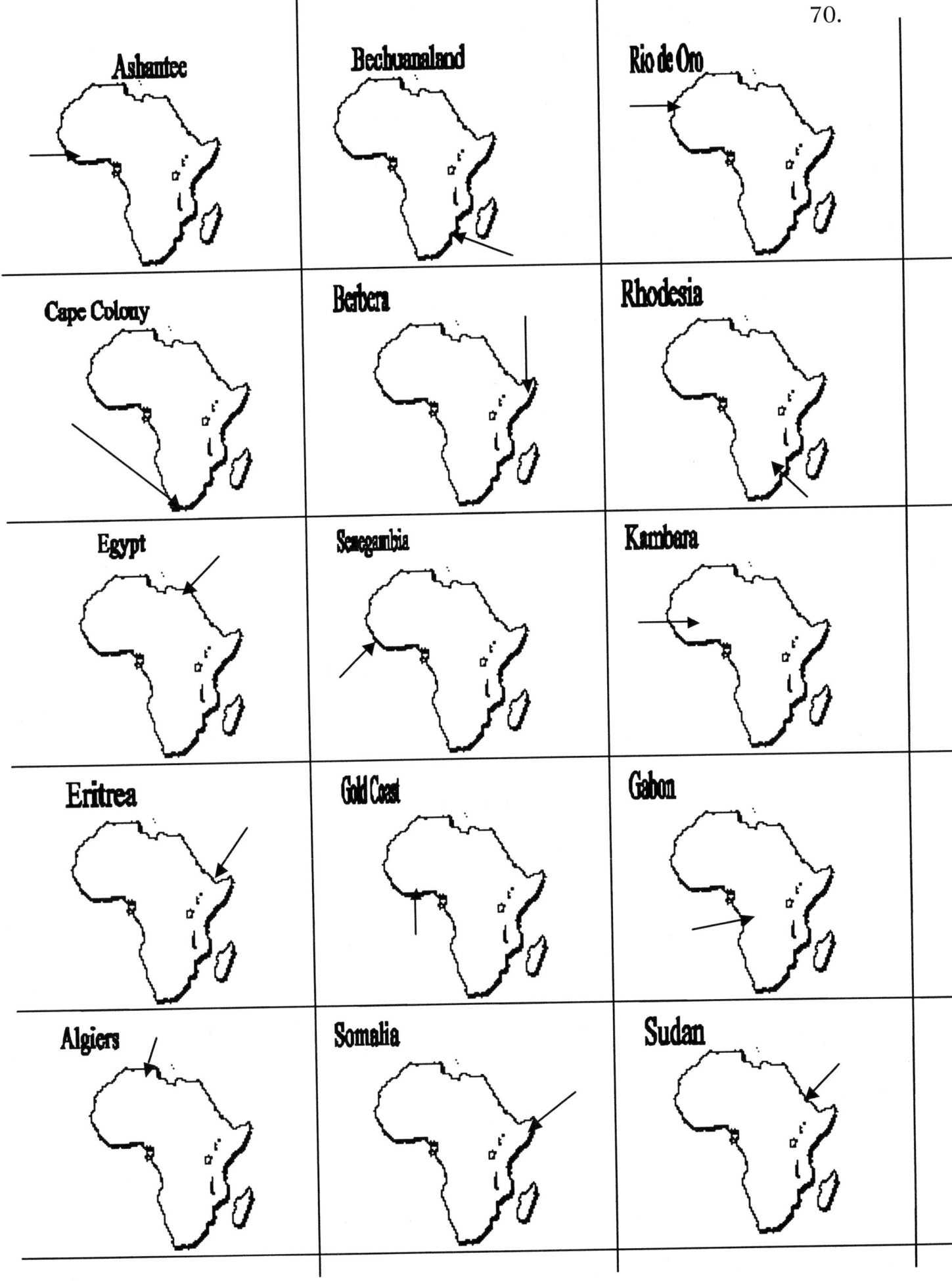

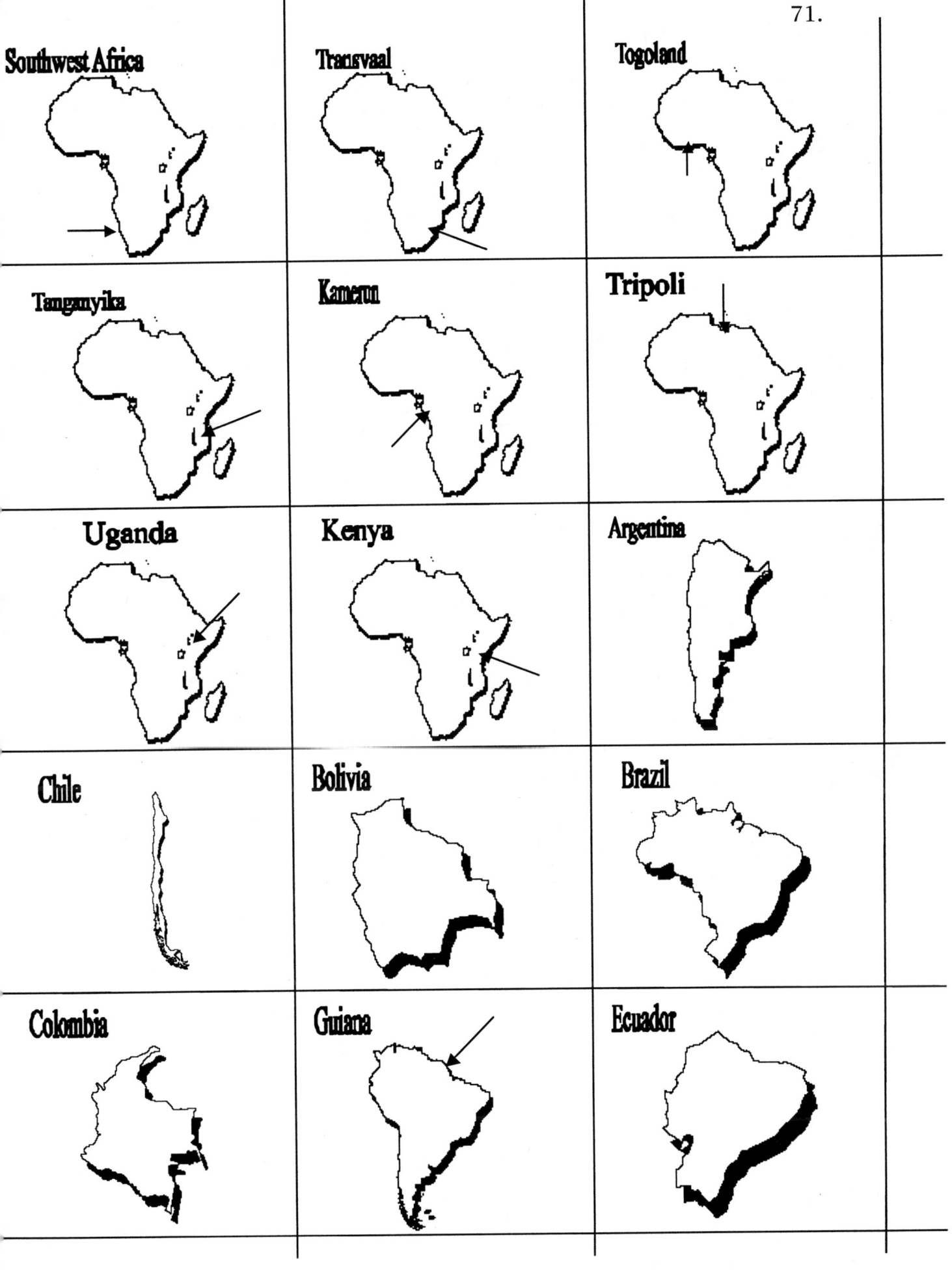

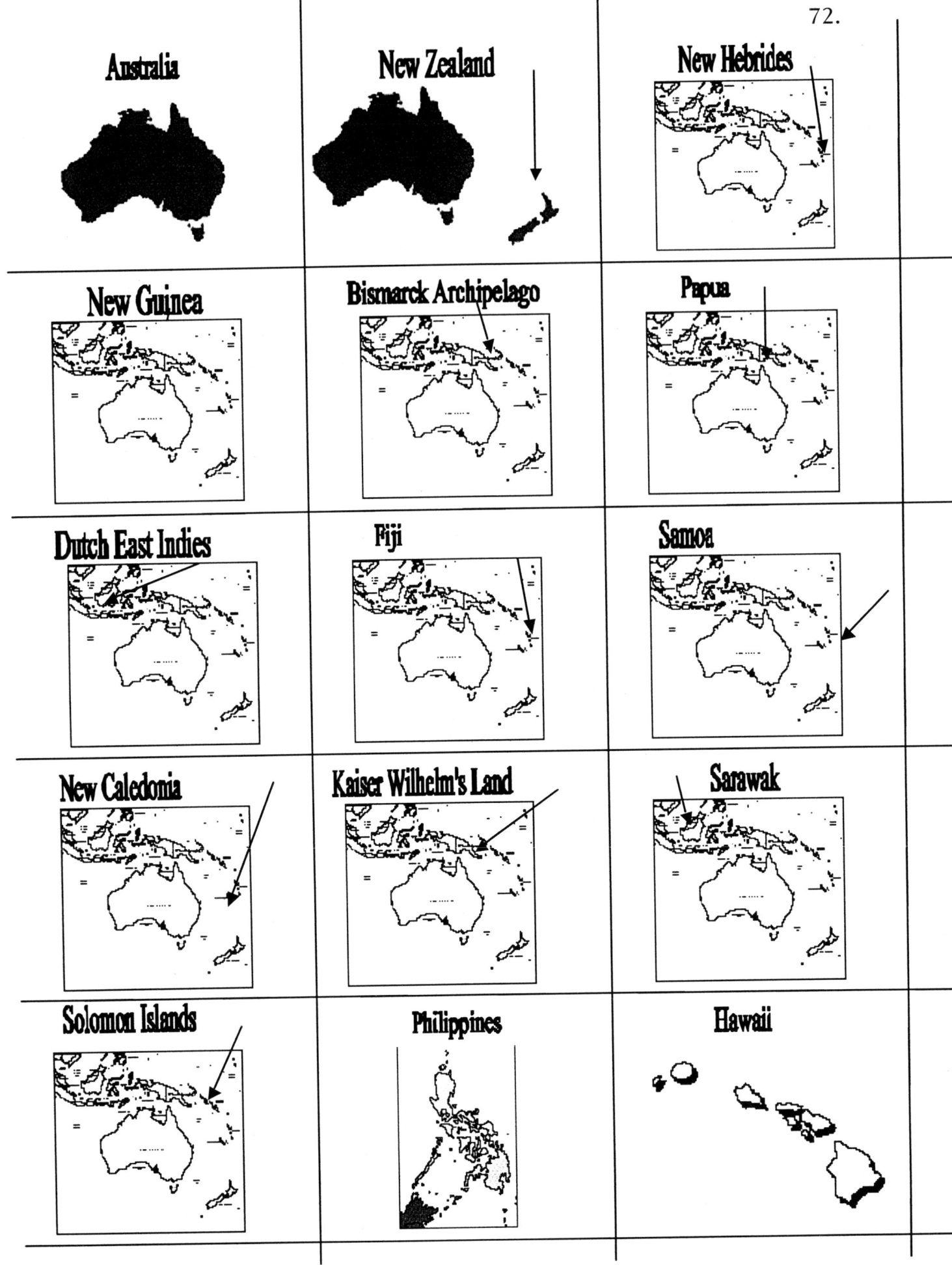

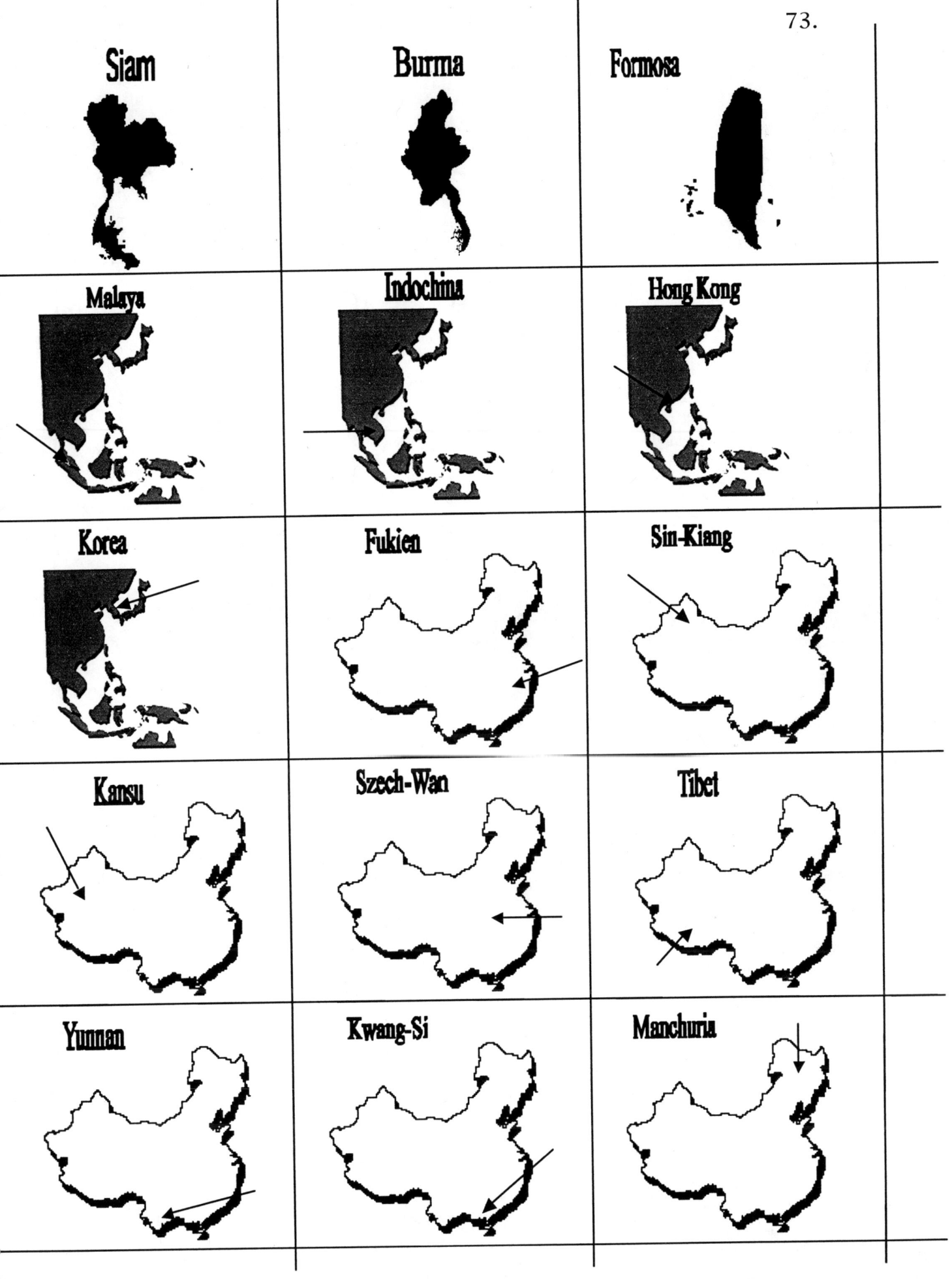

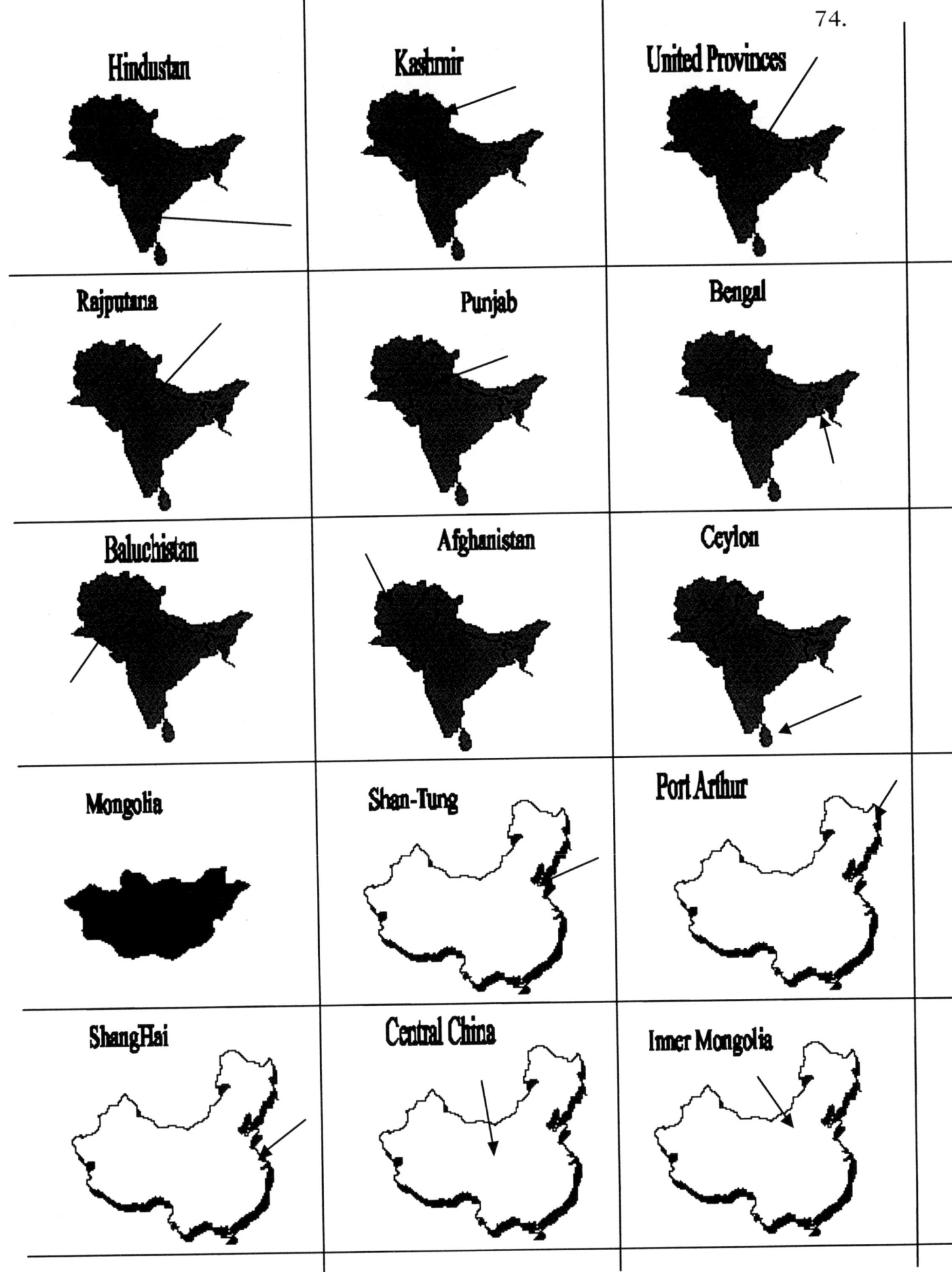

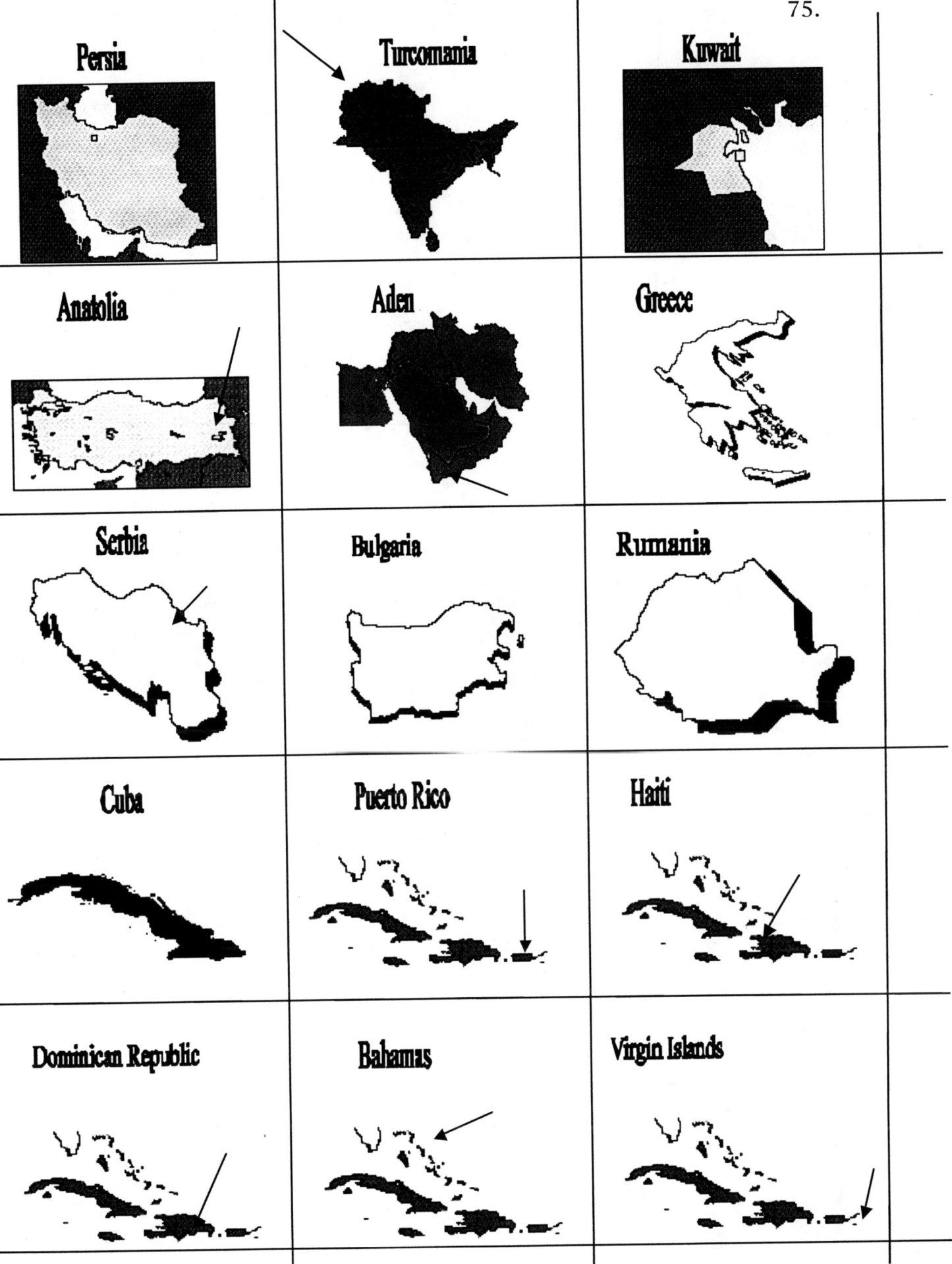

76.

Uruguay	Panama	Peru
Nicaragua	Mexico	Paraguay
Venezuela	British Honduras	Costa Rica
Jamaica	Honduras	El Salvador
Lesser Antilles	Falkland Islands	Panama

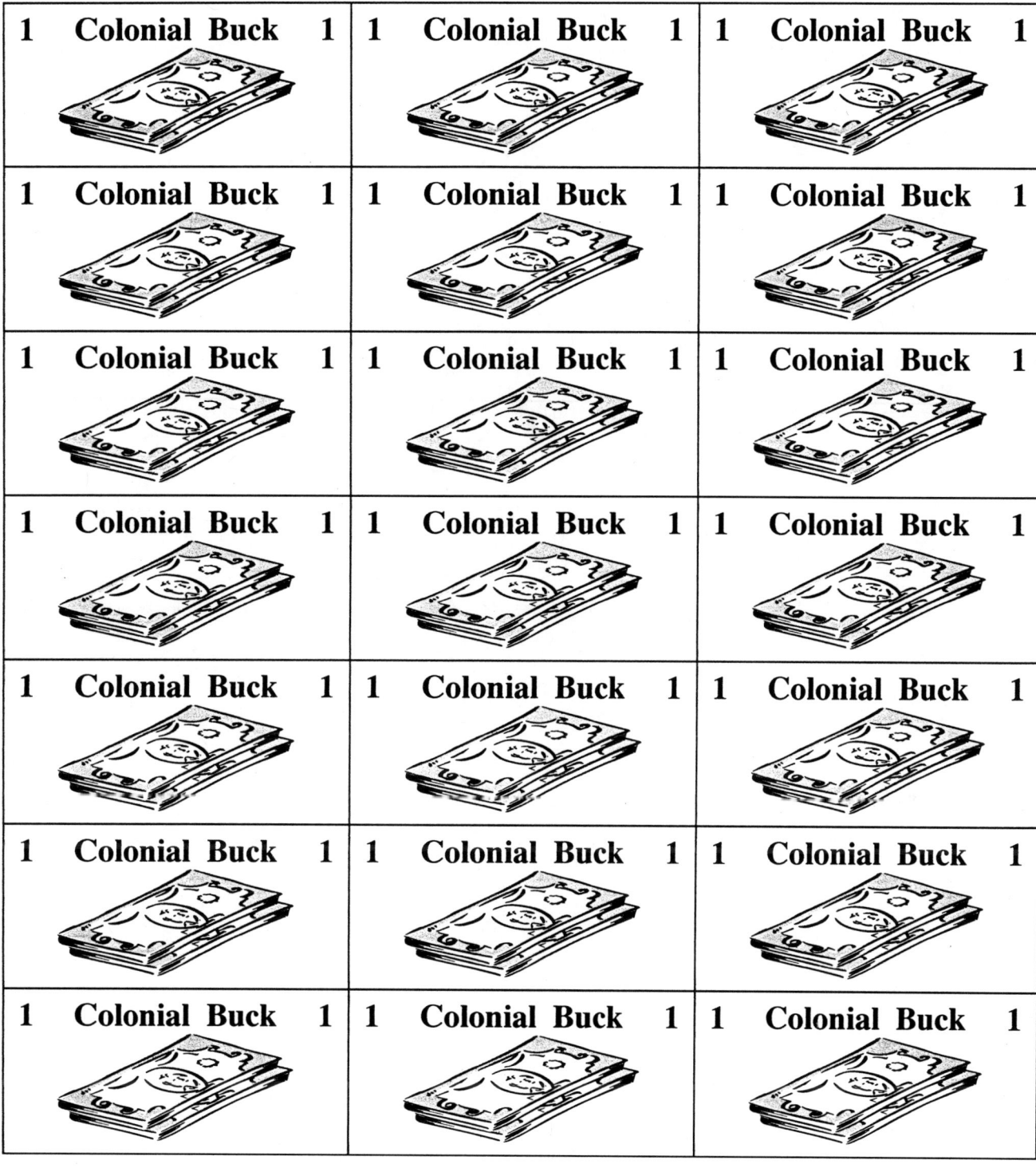

W.W. II Debates Teacher's Guide

Objective: To understand the various controversies surrounding W.W.II both at the time and today.

Duration: At least 1 class period for the research. From 1-15 class periods depending upon the number of topics debated.

Materials: Hand out a copy of the W.W. II Debates handout to everyone. A good research library with access to both primary and secondary sources is necessary. Use of the Internet may be helpful, but be very careful to explain that these sites may be very biased and not always accurate.

Procedure:
1. Divide the students into 2-4 member teams of mixed ability levels.

2. Divide the teams into those who will defend a particular side of the issue or the other.

3. Research the topics.

4. Conduct the debates in class with members of other teams judging those who are presenting.

Teacher Recommendations:
These debates require research and a great deal of preparation. What makes them a role-playing experience is that the debate team members must argue one side of the issue even if they disagree with it. Historical roles may be assigned which must be acted out by the students in character. In that case, they must speak as those people would have spoken and know only about things they could have known about in 1945.
If not, the teacher may decide to allow the students to use information from new research about these events as evidence. Either way, team members must defend their resolutions regardless of whether or not they are personally in agreement with it. The teacher and students together should decide what kind of debate format and rules will be used and how the project is to be judged or evaluated.

Debriefing:
1. What did you learn from this experience?
2. If W.W.II was so long ago, why are these issues still so controversial today?
3. Is there ever agreement on the truth of what really happened in history?
4. How did it feel to defend a position you might normally be against?
5. What other topics would you consider for debate?

W.W. II Debates

1. Was it really necessary for the United States to enter W.W.II? Could the United States have remained neutral? Were we dragged into the war or did we enter willingly?

2. Did President Roosevelt conspire to get the US to enter W.W.II even though many were opposed to it? What actions did he take to prevent or join the war?

3. Was the Japanese attack on Pearl Harbor truly a "surprise attack"? Did the United States have any advanced warning of the attack? What could we have done to avoid it?

4. Was it necessary to place Japanese-Americans in internment camps during W.W.II? Should damages be paid to survivors of those camps? What about the Italian and German-Americans? Why weren't they detained?

5. Could the US have done more to prevent the Holocaust from happening in Nazi Germany? Did we act quickly enough or in the appropriate ways?

6. Was it necessary to drop the atomic bombs on Hiroshima and Nagasaki? Could the war have been brought to end in any other way at that time?

7. Was it necessary to insist upon unconditional surrender from the Japanese at the end of W.W.II?

8. Was the use of carpet bombing against our enemies in W.W.II necessary and ethical?

9. Did the United States treat the Soviet Union as an equal partner in W.W.II? Did our handling of the demands of the Soviets at the end of W.W.II lead to the poor relations that would develop into the Cold War? Did Roosevelt and Truman deal with Stalin properly?

10. What happened to the body of Adolf Hitler? How did he really die? Are the bones in the possession of the Russians authentic? What of the conspiracy theories claiming he survived the Fall of Berlin and went into hiding?

11. Should Japan apologize for its actions in W.W.II? Should compensation be paid to the citizens of its former colonies? Who is responsible and who should pay?

80.

12. Should the personal property and money confiscated by the Nazis from Jews be returned to the survivors of the Holocaust and their descendants today? What if the funds were hidden in secret Swiss bank accounts that no one has claimed in all these years?

13. Should land occupied at the end of W.W.II by the victorious Allies be returned to the nations that lost them? Should they remain American or be given independence instead? Should Allied forces be completely withdrawn from countries occupied after W.W.II?

14. Should Nazi war criminals continue to be prosecuted and tried? If convicted, what kind of punishments should they be given?

15. What should be done about the Neo-Nazi movements in Germany and America? What about those who deny that the Holocaust ever took place?

Cold War Simulation Teacher's Guide

Objective: This simulation gives students a feel for the multiple levels of competition between the Superpowers during the Cold War. It helps them to realize that the way that the Cold War ended in the real world was not a foregone conclusion by any means.

Duration: 1-3 class periods.

Materials: Hand out a copy of the Cold War Simulation rules handout to everyone. Use a large world map that all can see. The pull down type is the best for visual effect, but any Cold War era world map could be made into a transparency for the game. Mark Communist countries and allies with a red sticker and those that were pro-USA in blue. Make sure that they are the kind that are easily removable like those round price stickers that they sell for garage sales. Start by marking the Superpowers and their staunchest allies circa 1945 and then add new stickers as countries declare for one camp or the other. The awesome sight of the whole world quickly filling up with colored stickers will give them a good sense for the geopolitics of the struggle and let them see where their next move should be.
Reproducible game pieces are provided at the end of this section of the book. Feel free to make as many as you need. It is a good idea to have several dozen of each kind cut out and stored in separate envelopes before the game. It is also very helpful to designate a couple of students to help you hand out and collect pieces during the game.

Procedure:
1. Divide the students into three teams, The United States, The Soviet Union, and the nonaligned countries. (Approximately 5 minutes).

2. Teams plan their moves according to the rules of the simulation. (Approximately 5 minutes).

3. Teams negotiate with each other. (Approximately 5-10 minutes).

4. The teacher records students' moves on the map. (Approximately 5 minutes).

5. Resolve conflicts according to the rules of the simulation. Make any changes on the map that arise from wars. (Approximately 5 minutes).

6. Repeat the above steps until there is a winner or all of the teams have been eliminated. (See victory conditions in the rules that follow).

7. Debrief. (Approximately 5-10 minutes).

Teacher Recommendations:
1. Three groups are created by teacher's choice or at random. The neutral or nonaligned countries are the toughest to play because they may require a bit of prior knowledge to play in some cases. Some pre-reading on the subject or research by players on their countries could enhance the game. For the most part they just need to listen to both sides equally and support the side that promises them the most. Try and get them to think like the country they are playing. They do not want to be left out of the gift giving by the superpowers or left without allies if a war breaks out, but would like to stay neutral if at all possible. The best model is modern India, which has received aid from both, but never firmly committed to either the East or the West. For the purposes of this game, neutral countries do not grow economically, they merely seek aid. They do not gain armies unless they conquer a neighbor or receive aid from a superpower. They usually do not activate their military forces unless attacked. They can not buy new armies or navies each turn and never develop nuclear forces on their own. If a neutral attacks another neutral of equal military strength the results are inconclusive unless they receive additional military aid from a superpower. The war continues to the next turn at which point either superpower may choose to intervene. For simplicity's sake some smaller nations have been combined into regions to increase playability, but it should be explained to students that in the real world even the tiniest neighbors might still be antagonists.

2. Caution students that the point of the game is to gain as much advantage over the other side as possible without being dragged into a war. If the Cold War turns into a "hot war" then everybody loses.

3. Coach the students on the various roles they can play within the group. This will help those less familiar with role-playing know what to do. Make sure everyone understands terms like hawk and dove before you begin.

4. The pace of the game will advance quickly once everyone grasps the concept. There are many ways to beat your opponent with war being only the last resort. Should a war actually break out then the Superpower that starts it must state whether it is a conventional war or nuclear. Simply list the country on the board that started it and the country that is being attacked (even if it was a neutral country that attacked another neutral country). Then ask who would like to declare for each side. Allow a few minutes to allow reluctant stragglers to commit or stay neutral and for some countries to change sides at the last minute if they wish. (This often happens in real wars). Once this is done, count up the number of armies, navies, and nuclear bombs and write them on the board in separate columns. The first force to be dealt with is the nuclear bombs the defender takes the first hits and then the attacker. (See rules for nuclear combat below). The country whose capitol is destroyed is immediately out for the rest of the game and any others subsequently attacked. Sometimes this will shock others into making peace and other times nations will fight on to the bitter end to seek revenge even if they know it means their own destruction. After any nuclear conflicts have been resolved the rest of the combat is resolved with conventional forces. Simply remove forces from each column as they cancel each other out. The side with the most forces remaining wins. If no side has a clear victory, the conflict goes on for another turn. If one side has only navies left and the other side has no forces left the navies may be converted into marines and invade in the same way as armies except at half strength.

Debriefing:

1. How real did this feel? Are you glad it turned out the way it did or terrified of the prospect? What would the world be like today if it had?

2. Why do you suppose the two superpowers felt they needed to compete in every area? What did they think would happen if they would lose?

3. Which of these areas of competition were tried in the actual Cold War and why? Which ones were most successful?

4. Who has the advantage at the beginning of the game? Who do you think usually wins? Who won the real Cold War? Why?

5. What would the world be like if the Cold War were still going on today?

Cold War Simulation

Purpose of the game: to understand the nature of competition between the Soviet Union and the U.S. during the Cold War.

Sequence of Play:
1. The US starts out with 75 points and the USSR 65. The teacher rolls one random event for each superpower on the random events chart and adjusts the map or point totals accordingly.
2. Each team chooses how their income will be spent. Deduct the number of income points spent from the total. A Superpower may purchase tokens that represent economic, food or military aid, to be given away to neutral countries. These tokens will later be distributed to neutral countries to gain their support. The Superpowers may also choose to spend their points on internal improvements that are listed below. Superpowers must spend all of their points each turn, but undistributed tokens may be spent on themselves.
3. After discussing among your team your choices for distribution, submit them in writing to the teacher. All moves are turned in simultaneously and take effect immediately. Once they are written down they cannot be changed. Each turn represents one year.
4. As countries declare their alliances place control markers of the appropriate color on the map and adjust the point totals and income for each superpower for the following year.

Rules:
There are three teams, The United States, The Soviet Union, and the nonaligned countries. The US and the USSR try to sway the neutral countries to their alliance to achieve world domination. This can be done through giving them economic, food or military aid, or by military conquest. The Superpowers may designate the number of tokens of each kind that they wish to give to a neutral nation. Those points are no longer part of that nations total. When a country agrees to become an ally of a superpower their strength points get added to the superpowers total. This number is also printed on that nation or region's card. Each country has a given number of economic, food or military aid points it desires before committing to one side or the other. This is printed on that nation or region's card. These numbers are merely goals however, the nation may agree to commit to one side or the other at any time they wish.

Domestic spending options for the Superpowers:

1. **Internal Development.** Each point invested in economic power increases the nation's income by one point the following turn and every turn thereafter. This is done by purchasing economic aid cards and spending them on your own country.

2. **The Arms Race.** These conventional military forces are the same as military aid cards but are retained by the superpower for use at home and abroad. They come in two types: armies or navies. A superpower must have at least one navy to deploy forces on another continent. One navy is needed for each new continent that may not be reached from your home country by land. Military power may be used in a conventional war against any country. If their defensive strength is overwhelmed the country becomes a satellite. If the other superpower tries to take the same country in the same year, a civil war breaks out, and the forces fight until there is a victor. Each turn new forces may be added. At any time a superpower may decide to withdraw or escalate the conflict to a nuclear one. Use of nuclear force removes a neutral country or region from the game permanently and may provoke a nuclear war with the other superpower if it has vowed to protect it.

3. **Nuclear arms.** Each nuclear arm purchased can be used to destroy the capital city of one country. A destroyed country is then out of the game. The other superpower may choose to retaliate with everything that they have by launching a nuclear attack of any kind, anywhere. If a superpower is the victim of an attack, they may only respond with 90% of their forces because some of their forces would be destroyed in the initial attack.

4. **The Space Race.** A country must invest in the space race if it wishes to build Intercontinental Ballistic Missiles. Each point spent on the space race increases your economy by one point.
1 card = long range bombers. Your country may now drop atomic bombs by air. This means that its planes may still be shot down by the enemy's conventional forces, however.
2 cards = rockets. You may use them to destroy the army of a neighboring country or deliver an atomic bomb to destroy their capitol
3 cards = medium range missiles. You may use them to destroy the army of any country on the same continent as you are or deliver an atomic bomb to destroy their capitol.
4 cards = long range missiles. You may use them to destroy the army of any country in the world or deliver an atomic bomb to destroy their capitol.

5 cards = moon landing. You are the envy of the whole world! Gain one free economic aid card, one free military aid card and add +1 to your economy.

6 cards = missile defense system. You may destroy one incoming enemy missile for each additional space card purchased from now on.

Victory Conditions:
The first superpower to reach 150 points or eliminate the other superpower wins the game. The neutral countries can win if both superpowers have been wiped out and they are still intact. It is possible for everyone to win if a nuclear war has been avoided and no countries have been destroyed. It is also possible for everyone to lose if a nuclear war has occurred and all countries have been destroyed.

Roles on a team:
Individuals on each team will play one of the following roles:

A. War hawk: pro-military, eager for a confrontation, looking for a showdown.

B. Doves: believe in peace at all costs, do not like war under any circumstances, especially fearful of nuclear war.

C. Diplomats: will always try to negotiate a compromise with the other superpower or try to persuade neutral countries to join your side.

D. Scientists: will try to advance knowledge of space.

E. Isolationists: are in favor of staying out of other countries' business.

F. Businessmen: want to have peace to trade with other countries, but like to sell things to the military too. Support whatever helps your nation's income.

G. Farmers: want countries where they can sell their food. They will sell food to just about any country they can.

H. Reformers: want to improve things at home first. Feel that wars are a waste of money.

I. Dissidents: people who are unhappy with their own government. They like the other superpower better and can be persuaded to defect to the other side, but it is usually more fun to stay home and complain all the time.

J. Patriots: people who love their country and feel that it can do no wrong. They have a hard time understanding why everybody doesn't want to be like them.

Random Events Table: Roll a 20-sided die

1- new invention	+1 economic point
2- technology becomes outdated	-1 economic point
3- bumper crop	gain 1 food aid token
4- crop failure	lose 1 food aid token
5- epidemic	-1 economic point
6- medical breakthrough	+1 economic point
7- revolution in neutral country of teacher's choice	reroll: 1-10 it becomes an ally of the US, 11-20 an ally of the USSR
8- revolt in neutral country or region of teacher's choice	lose 1 ally
9- labor unrest	-1 economic point
10- increase in productivity	+1 economic point
11- civil unrest	lose one military aid token
12- patriotic movement	gain one free military aid token
13- strong leader	+1 economic point and gain one free economic aid token
14- weak leader	-1 economic point and lose one free economic aid token
15- shortages/inflation	-1 economic point
16- surpluses/deflation	-1 economic point
17- scandal	lose one economic aid token
18- reform movement	gain one economic aid token
19- crime/drug problem	-1 economic point
20- law and order movement	+1 economic point

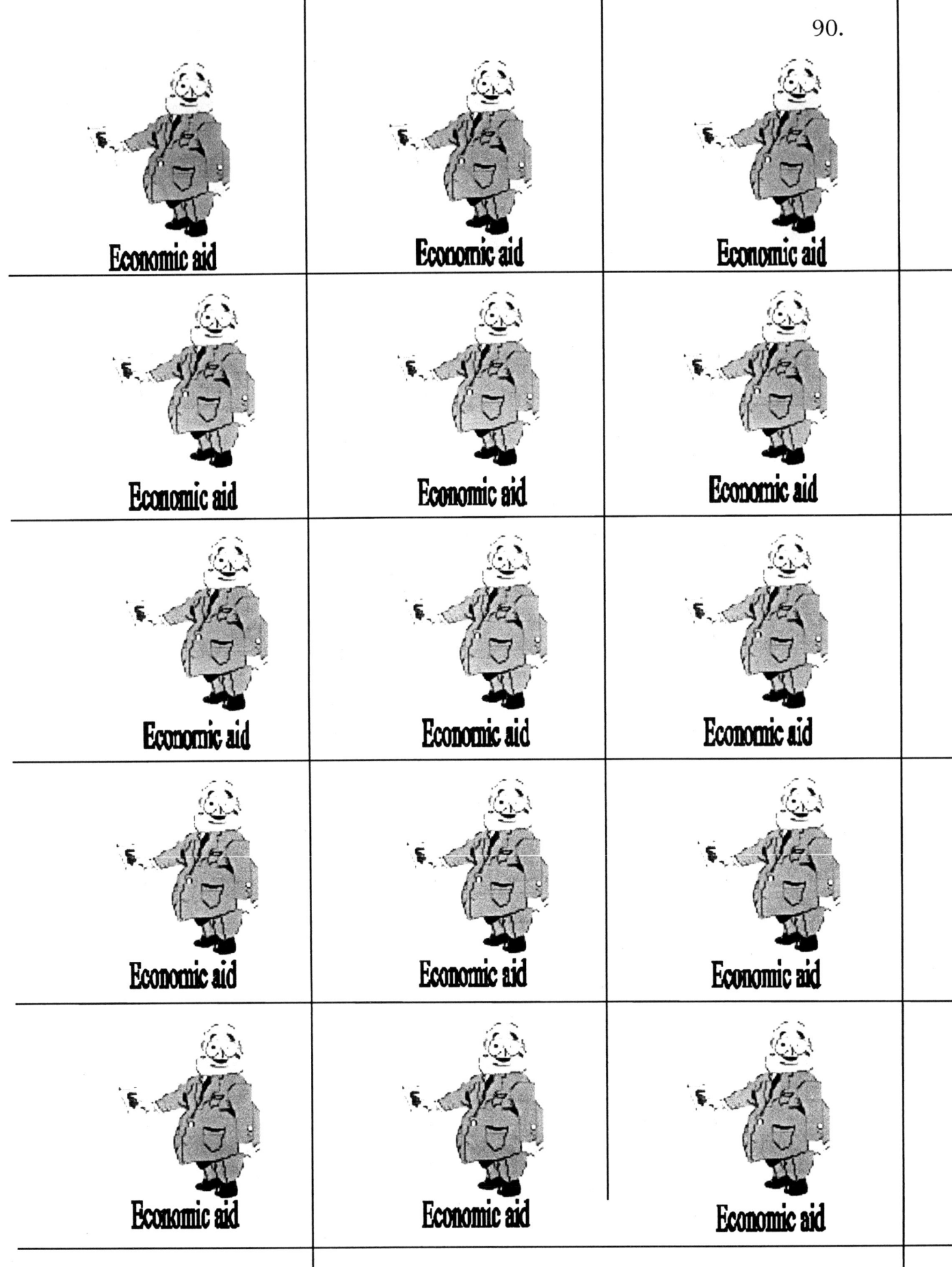

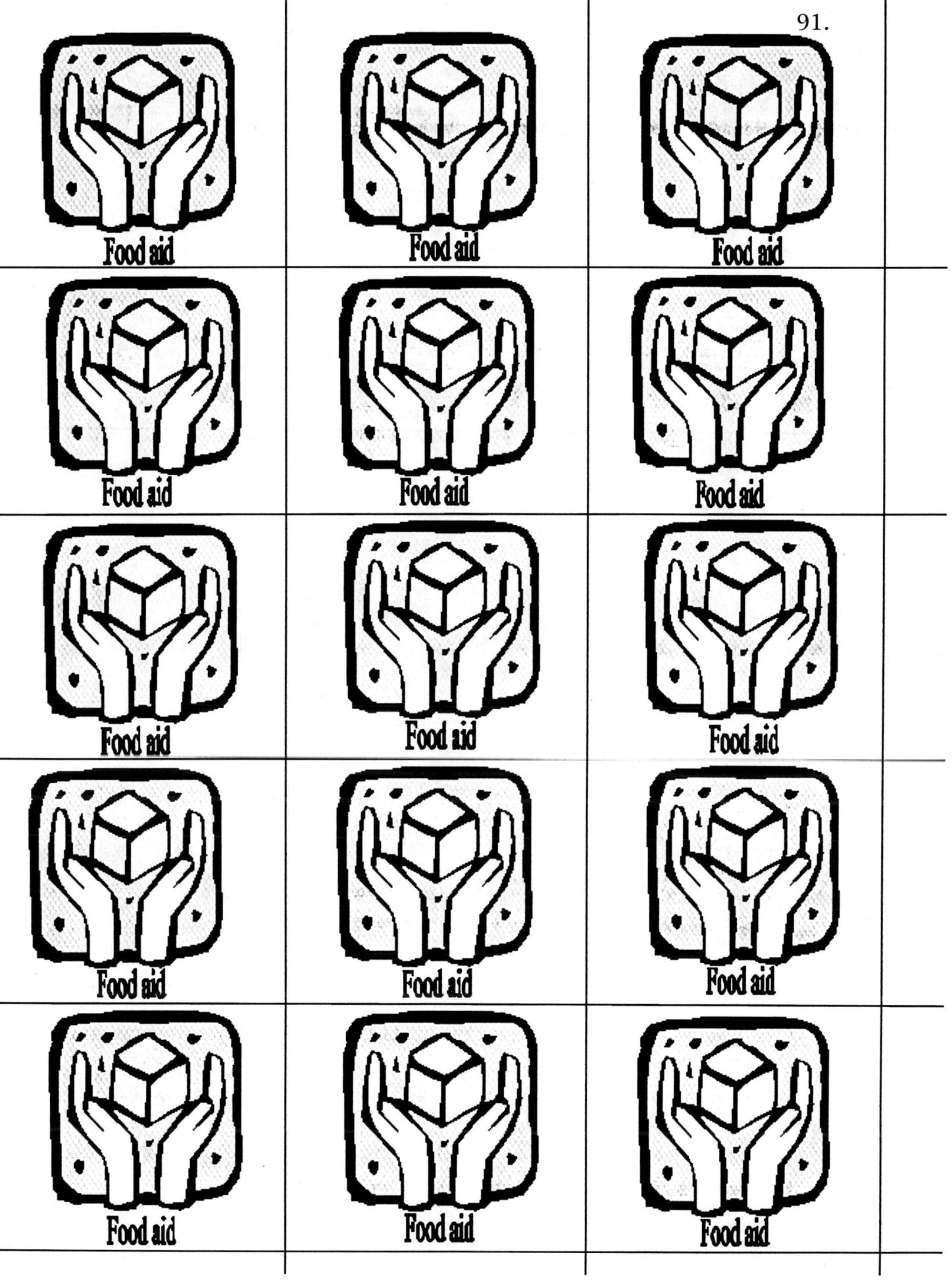

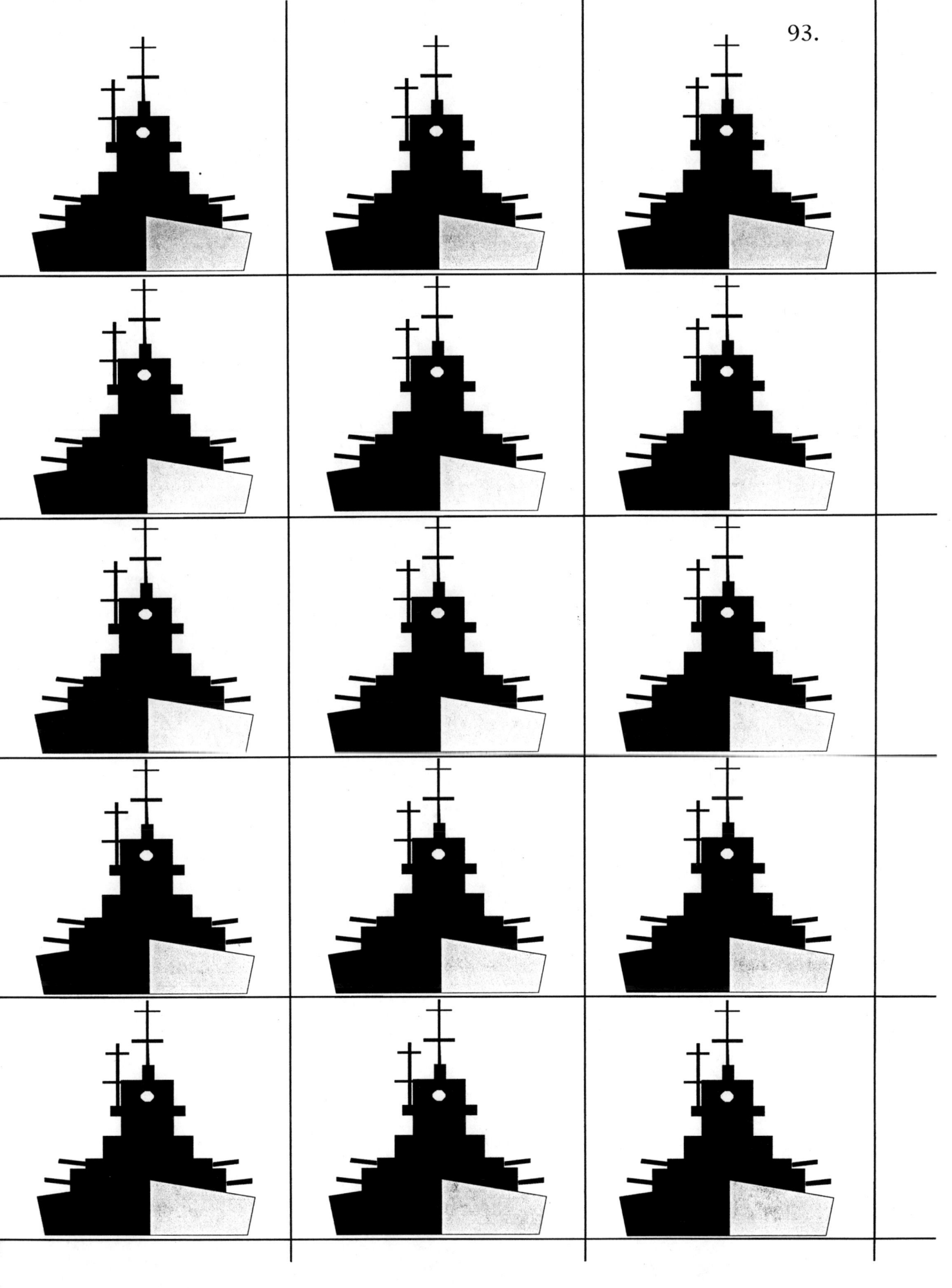

Nuclear bomb	Nuclear bomb	Nuclear bomb
Nuclear bomb	Nuclear bomb	Nuclear bomb
Nuclear bomb	Nuclear bomb	Nuclear bomb
Nuclear bomb	Nuclear bomb	Nuclear bomb
Nuclear bomb	Nuclear bomb	Nuclear bomb

95.

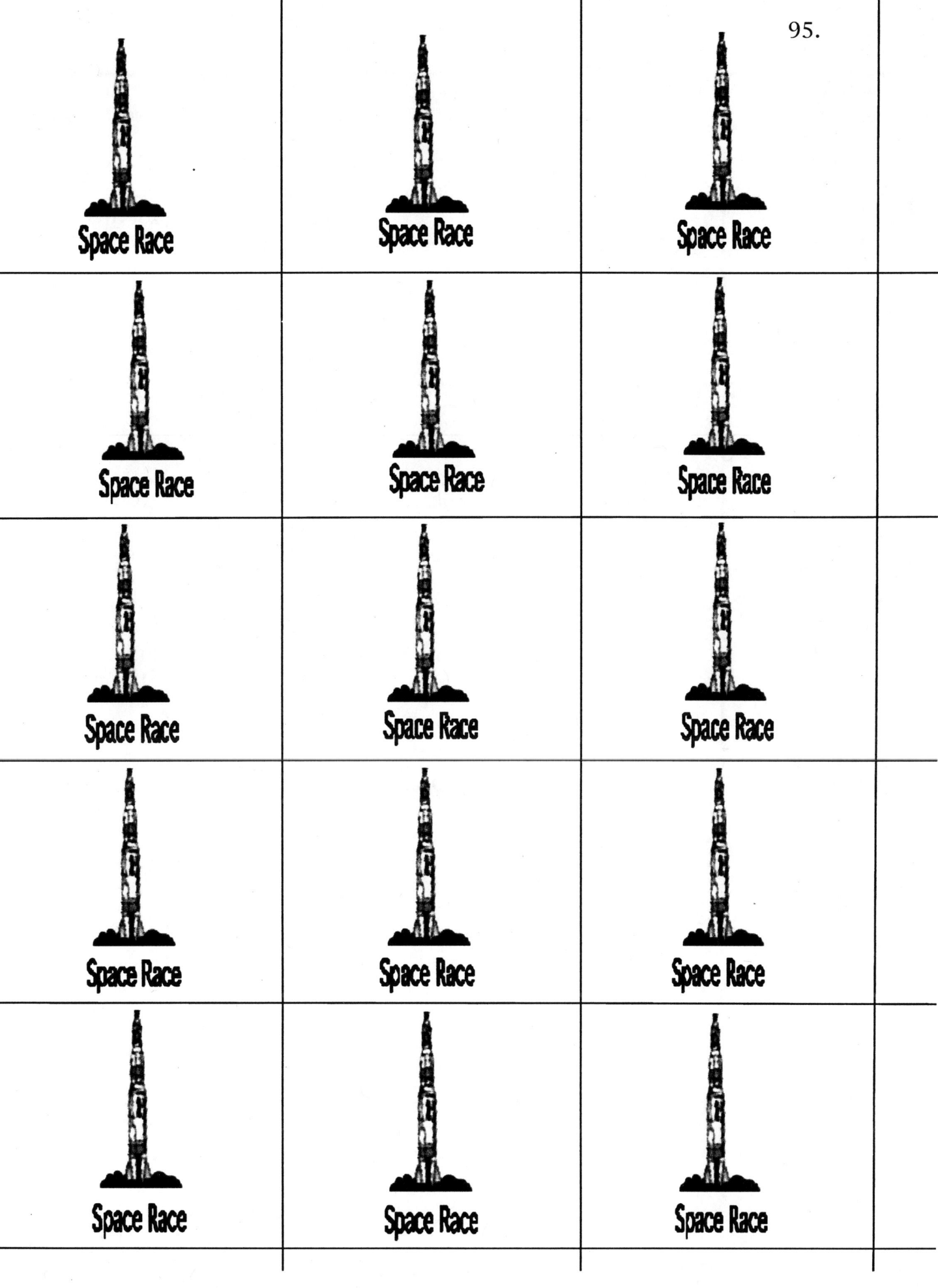

Country: India Location: Asia Goals: economic: 5 food: 5 military: 5 Strength: 5	Country: Afghanistan Location: Asia Goals: economic: 1 food: 1 military: 1 Strength: 2	Country: Pakistan Location: Asia Goals: economic: 3 food: 1 military: 4 Strength: 4	Country: Iran Location: Asia Goals: economic: 2 food: 1 military: 4 Strength: 4	Country: Iraq Location: Middle East Goals: economic: 2 food: 1 military: 2 Strength: 3
Region: West Africa Countries: Ghana, Nigeria, Dahomey, Upper Volta, Ivory Coast, Liberia, Sierra Leone, Guinea & others Goals: economic: 5 food: 5 military: 3 Strength: 5	Region: Southeast Asia Countries: Thailand, Malaysia, Singapore & Brunei Goals: economic: 2 food: 3 military: 1 Strength: 3	Country: Israel Location: Middle East Goals: economic: 2 food: 1 military: 4 Strength: 2	Region: Arabia Countries: Saudi Arabia, Yemen, Oman, Kuwait, Bahrain, UAE & Qatar Location: Middle East Goals: economic: 1 food: 1 military: 5 Strength: 6	Region: Southern Asia Countries: Burma, Bangladesh, Nepal, & Bhutan Location: Asia Goals: economic: 2 food: 4 military: 1 Strength: 3
Country: Indonesia Location: Asia Goals: economic: 4 food: 3 military: 2 Strength: 2	Region: Indochina Countries: Vietnam, Laos, & Cambodia Goals: economic: 3 food: 3 military: 3 Strength: 3	Region: Oceania Countries: Australia, New Zealand, Papua New Guinea, Fiji, Samoa & others Goals: economic: 1 food: 2 military: 2 Strength: 4	Region: The Sahara Countries: Morocco, Algeria, Tunisia, Libya, Mali, Chad, Niger, & Mauritania Goals: economic: 4 food: 4 military: 1 Strength: 3	Region: Horn of Africa Countries: Sudan, Ethiopia, Djibouti, & Somalia Goals: economic: 4 food: 5 military: 4 Strength: 4

Country: Philippines Location: Asia Goals: economic: 4 food: 4 military: 3 Strength: 2	Country: Taiwan Location: Asia Goals: economic: 2 food: 1 military: 5 Strength: 3	Region: Central America Countries: Guatemala, El Salvador, Honduras, Belize & Nicaragua Goals: economic: 4 food: 4 military: 4 Strength: 2	Region: The Congo Countries: Zaire, Congo, Gabon, Equatorial Guinea, Sao Tome & Principe, Cameroon, & Central Afr. Rep. Goals: economic: 5 food: 4 military: 4 Strength: 3	Country: Egypt Location: Africa Goals: economic: 3 food: 1 military: 5 Strength: 5
Country: Sweden Location: Europe Goals: economic: 1 food: 0 military: 1 Strength: 3	Country: Finland Location: Europe Goals: economic: 1 food: 0 military: 1 Strength: 2	Country: Yugoslavia Location: Europe Goals: economic: 3 food: 1 military: 3 Strength: 2	Country: Spain Location: Europe Goals: economic: 2 food: 0 military: 1 Strength: 2	Country: Portugal Location: Europe Goals: economic: 1 food: 0 military: 2 Strength: 2
Country: Mexico Location: Central America Goals: economic: 5 food: 1 military: 1 Strength: 2	Country: Panama Location: Central America Goals: economic: 3 food: 1 military: 3 Strength: 1	Country: Cuba Location: Caribbean Goals: economic: 4 food: 1 military: 3 Strength: 2	Country: Colombia Location: South America Goals: economic: 3 food: 1 military: 2 Strength: 2	Country: Chile Location: South America Goals: economic: 3 food: 1 military: 2 Strength: 3

Region: Northern South America Countries: Venezuela, Surinam, Guyana Goals: economic: 3 food: 3 military: 1 Strength: 4	Region: Southern Africa Countries: South Africa, Zambia, Mozambique, Rhodesia, Lesotho, & Swaziland Goals: economic: 3 food: 2 military: 4 Strength: 4	Region: Eastern Africa Countries: Madagascar, Tanzania, Kenya, Mozambique, Malawi, Rwanda, & Burundi Goals: economic: 4 food: 4 military: 4 Strength: 3	Region: Caribbean Countries: Haiti, Dominican Republic, Bahamas, Jamaica & others Location: Caribbean Goals: economic: 4 food: 4 military: 1 Strength: 3	Region: The Levant Countries: Lebanon, Jordan, & Syria Goals: economic: 3 food: 1 military: 4 Strength: 6
Country: Paraguay Location: South America Goals: economic: 1 food: 1 military: 1 Strength: 1	Country: Brazil Location: South America Goals: economic: 4 food: 1 military: 2 Strength: 4	Country: Ecuador Location: South America Goals: economic: 1 food: 1 military: 1 Strength: 1	Country: Peru Location: South America Goals: economic: 2 food: 2 military: 2 Strength: 2	Country: Bolivia Location: South America Goals: economic: 1 food: 1 military: 2 Strength: 2
Country: Argentina Location: South America Goals: economic: 2 food: 2 military: 3 Strength: 3	Country: Uruguay Location: South America Goals: economic: 1 food: 1 military: 1 Strength: 1	Country: China Location: East Asia Goals: economic: 5 food: 6 military: 5 Strength: 10		

World History Counterfactuals: "What if...?" Teacher's Guide

Objective: These are series of interesting critical thinking questions that encourage students to think about the possibilities of alternative outcomes in history and their consequences.

Duration: A few minutes-1 class period.

Materials: Write the question(s) for the day on the board or print them onto an overhead transparency.

Procedure:

These questions may be used to evoke student participation during a lecture, begin a class discussion or debate, or as a writing prompt for journal writing or essays.

Teacher Recommendations:

There is a really fun Internet newsgroup called "soc.history.what-if" where learned scholars and history buffs alike post messages endlessly about all kinds of speculative and alternative historical outcomes. For those who don't know what a newsgroup is, it is an electronic message board that is accessible through most Internet providers. If you can't find it on your Internet provider software, read the documentation that came with it or ask them for help. You are usually given the option to read the newsgroup or subscribe to it. If you are only visiting, choose "read messages" if you plan to go back again and again choose subscribe to newsgroup. Keep in mind that it is not a chat group, so don't expect any instant responses to your question. You must go back and check periodically to see if anyone wrote an answer to your question. After a certain period of time, old messages are deleted, so don't wait too long. Try it out some time with your classes; it really can be a great discussion starter or writing prompt. As with any Internet newsgroup, caution your students that they may come across the occasional loony out there in cyberspace, but since the group is well-moderated they usually get ridiculed by the more responsible members and quickly drop out. The only other word of caution is that if a student asks a question which has come up many times before, they may get teased as being a "newbie". Usually the best thing to do is apologize, admit you are new, and then ask the group to respond anyway. It is always a good idea to read the Frequently Asked Questions (FAQ's) for a newsgroup to avoid doing something that will embarrass you or annoy people.

Debriefing:

1. Ask students to create follow up questions of their own.
2. Write an essay or journal entry on their own follow up questions.
3. Post your questions on the soc.history.what-if newsgroup to see what kinds of responses your class gets.

Ancient History Questions:

1. What if the cradle of western civilization had been in Europe?
2. What if the cradle of western civilization had been in Africa?
3. What if agriculture had never been invented?
4. What if cities had never been invented?
5. What if the alphabet had never been invented?
6. What if writing had never been invented?
7. What if monotheism had never been invented?
8. What if Moses had never lived?
9. What if Christ had never lived?
10. What if the scientific discoveries of the Greeks had continued?
11. What if Socrates had never lived?
12. What if the Greek city-states had united?
13. What if Alexander the Great had never lived?
14. What if Alexander the Great had not died young?
15. What if Alexander the Great had reached China?
16. What if Alexander the Great had turned westward instead of attacking the Persian Empire?
17. What if Caesar had never lived?
18. What if Caesar had been killed in battle in Gaul?
19. What if Caesar had not been assassinated?
20. What if Augustus had never lived?
21. What if Augustus had lost the civil war?
22. What if Constantine had not moved the capital of the Roman Empire to Byzantium?
23. What if the Roman Empire never fell?
24. What if the Roman Empire had discovered America?
25. What if the Roman Empire had conquered the rest of Africa?
26. What if the Roman Empire had conquered China?
27. What if the Roman Empire had conquered India?
28. What if the Roman Empire had conquered the Germanic tribes?
29. What if the Roman Empire had discovered gunpowder?
30. What if ancient India had been united?
31. What if ancient India did not have a caste system?
32. What if ancient India had recorded history in the same way the west did?
33. What if ancient China had recorded history in the same way the west did?
34. What if ancient China had been a democracy?
35. What if ancient China had an alphabet?
36. What if the horse had not become extinct in North America?
37. What if ancient Americans had discovered metallurgy?
38. What if ancient Americans had discovered the wheel?
39. What if ancient Americans had discovered Europe or Asia?
40. What if ancient Americans had developed nation states?

Medieval Questions:

1. What if the papacy had arisen in another city besides Rome?
2. What if the Great Schism had never occurred?
3. What if the Arabs had converted to Christianity?
4. What if the Mongols had never left Mongolia?
5. What if Attila the Hun had never been born?
6. What if Genghis Khan had never been born?
7. What if the Vikings had stayed in America?
8. What if the Vikings had told other Europeans about America?
9. What if the Normans had not conquered England?
10. What if the Vikings had never converted to Christianity?
11. What if the Russians had never converted to Christianity?
12. What if Mohammed had never been born?
13. What if the Mongols had never conquered China?
14. What if the Mongols had conquered Japan?
15. What if the Mongols had conquered Europe?
16. What if the Mongols had remained united?
17. What if the Germanic tribes had united?
18. What if Charlemagne had never lived?
19. What if Charlemagne's heirs had preserved his kingdom?
20. What if the Arabs had conquered all of Europe?
21. What if medieval monks had not preserved the writings of the Greeks, Romans, and Arabs?
22. What if the Maya had not practiced human sacrifice?
23. What if the Maya had built a unified empire?
24. What if the Maya had discovered refrigeration?
25. What if the Japanese had built a unified empire?
26. What if the Tartars had not attacked the Russians?
27. What if the Crusader States had not fallen to the Turks?
28. What if the Jews had been allowed to return to the Holy Land?
29. What if a cure had been found for the bubonic plague?
30. What if the kingdoms of medieval Africa had made wider contact with the Europeans?

Renaissance Questions:

1. What if Renaissance Italy had been united?
2. What if the Pope had agreed to Martin Luther's reforms?
3. What if the Byzantine Empire had not fallen to the Turks?
4. What if the Italian explorers had claimed their discoveries for their own countries?
5. What if Germany had united at the same time as England and France?
6. What if Galileo had not gone blind?

Renaissance Questions (continued):

7. What if Galileo had been free to publish his ideas about the place of the earth in the universe?
8. What if Leonardo da Vinci had actually built some the inventions in his notebook such the helicopter, glider, or tank?
9. What if Shakespeare were Polish?
10. What if Lorenzo de Medici had lived after his denunciation by Savonarola?
11. What if Cortes had not conquered the Aztecs?
12. What if the Spanish had discovered gold in California?
13. What if Columbus had given up?
14. What if Columbus had been turned down by the Spanish?
15. What if Columbus had convinced the Portuguese to back his voyages of discovery?
16. What if Columbus had reached Asia?
17. What if Columbus had known he wasn't in Asia?
18. What if Magellan had lived to return to Spain?
19. What if Giovanni Caboto (John Cabot) had survived his second voyage?
20. What if the English or French had never claimed colonies in the New World?
21. What if the Native Americans had had resistance to European diseases?
22. What if the potato had not been discovered in the New World?
23. What if maize had not been discovered in the New World?
24. What if the French or Spanish had conquered all of North America?
25. What if the Scientific Revolution had taken place in China?
26. What if the Chinese had discovered America?
27. What if the Chinese had discovered the printing press with moveable type?
28. What if Henry VIII had been granted a divorce by the Pope?
29. What if the Spanish Armada had been victorious?
30. What if Francis Drake had been captured by the Spanish and hanged for piracy?
31. What if the Ivan the Terrible had been able to pick his own nickname to go down in the history books?
32. What if the Council of Florence had succeeded in reunifying the Roman Catholic and Orthodox churches?
33. What if Africans had developed guns before the Europeans?
34. What King Alfonso's ban on slavery had been enforced throughout Africa?
35. What if there had been no slavery in America?
36. What if tobacco never existed?
37. What if the New World never existed?
38. What if gunpowder had never been introduced to Europe?

Renaissance Questions (continued):

39. What if the Inquisition had never been carried out?
40. What if Protestantism had prevailed in Southern Europe?

The Age of Reason Questions:

1. What if Oliver Cromwell had been a Catholic?
2. What if Charles I had won the English Civil War?
3. What if James II had remained king in 1688?
4. What if Isaac Newton had never been born?
5. What if the works of the philosophes had been successfully repressed?
6. What if the Pope had become an enlightened monarch?
7. What if the French Revolution had occurred before the American Revolution?
8. What if the French had not aided the Americans in their Revolution?
9. What if Catherine the Great were not of German ancestry?
10. What if Peter the Great had not improved Russia's contacts with Western Europe?
11. What if the French Revolution had occurred during the reign of Louis XIV?
12. What if the English Revolution had been as violent as the French Revolution?
13. What if the French, Spanish, or Italians had tolerated Protestantism?
14. What if the revolutions had succeeded in Germany, Russia, Spain or other countries?
15. What if Louis XVI had been a stronger king?
16. What if Louis XVI had married a French woman instead of Marie Antoinette?
17. What if Adam Smith had been a communist?
18. What if one the parties of the French Revolution had become the permanent government and the revolution had ended peacefully?
19. What if Robespierre had stayed in power?
20. What if most of the reforms of the French Revolution had become permanent?
21. What if the French Revolution had been carried out by Communists?
22. What if Frederick the Great had not had a well-trained army?
23. What if the Thirty Years War had had a clear winner?
24. What if Napoleon had conquered Russia?
25. What if Napoleon had won at Waterloo?
26. What if Napoleon had not died young?
27. What if Napoleon had remained an Italian citizen?

The Age of Reason Questions (continued):

28. What if the Aborigines of Australia had remained isolated from the rest of the world?
29. What if Australia had been settled by a different country?
30. What if Australia had not been settled by prisoners?
31. What if the Polynesian islands had remained undiscovered?
32. What if France had prevailed in India and driven out the British?

Industrial Revolution Questions:

1. What if the Industrial Revolution had begun in another part of Europe other than England?
2. What if the refinement of petroleum had been discovered 100 or 200 years earlier?
3. What if the British had never found coal in their home country?
4. What if Britain had been self-sufficient in raw materials?
5. What if the British had had no overseas markets for their goods?
6. What if ways had been found to curb the pollution and waste of industrialism sooner?
7. What if labor laws had been introduced sooner?
8. What if there were no labor unions?
9. What if the railroad had not been invented?
10. What if the Bessemer Process had not been invented?
11. What if ways to improve the food supply had not been found?
12. What if modern medicine had not arrived to improve living conditions and extend life expectancy?
13. What if Thomas Malthus's predictions had been right?
14. What if the steam engine had been invented earlier?
15. What if the franchise had not been extended to the lower social classes in England?

Imperialism Questions:

1. What if Russia had never sold Alaska to the United States?
2. What if the United States had tried to gain colonies in Africa?
3. What if the United States had gone to war with Britain over Hawaii?
4. What if there were no gold or diamonds in South Africa?
5. What if the Boers had defeated the British in South Africa?
6. What if the Zulus had kept their lands in South Africa?
7. What if Egypt (or any other colony) had kept its independence?
8. What if the French had accomplished their goal of unifying all of North Africa under their colonial rule?
9. What if the Age of Imperialism were still going on today?
10. What if the Africans had developed or obtained modern guns prior to European attempts at Imperialism?

Imperialism Questions (continued):

11. What if Africans had united to resist Imperialism?
12. What if Europeans had ignored the Monroe Doctrine?
13. What if Europeans had ignored the Open Door Policy?
14. What if the British had been able to convert all of India to Christianity?
15. What if Russia had achieved its goals of access to the Mediterranean, Indian Ocean, or domination of the Balkans?

WWI Questions:

1. What if the Archduke Franz Ferdinand had lived?
2. What if the British had tanks at the beginning of WWI?
3. What if the Germans had used all of their battleships during the war?
4. What if Germany had only attacked France or Russia in WWI?
5. What if America had stayed neutral?
6. What if some of the neutral countries like Spain or Sweden had joined the war?
7. What if the Schlieffen Plan had worked?
8. What if the Russian Revolution had happened earlier?
9. What if the Russian Revolution had never happened?
10. What if Lenin had not returned to Russia?
11. What if Italy had not changed it alliances or stayed neutral?
12. What if the White army had won the Russian Civil War?
13. What if the Czar and his family had lived?
14. What if the Treaty of Versailles had been more lenient on the Central Powers?
15. What if the Ottoman Empire or Austro-Hungarian Empire had remained intact?

WWII Questions:

1. What if Mussolini had stayed a Socialist?
2. What if Mussolini had stayed neutral?
3. What if Mussolini had not been allied with Hitler?
4. What if Mussolini had been a better military planner? Could the Italian armed forces have performed better?
5. What if Hitler had had a more normal family life during his upbringing?
6. What if Hitler had been successful as an artist?
7. What if Hitler had been killed during WWI?
8. What if Hitler had been replaced as leader of the Nazi Party?
9. What if Mein Kampf had been a flop?
10. What if the Beer Hall Putsch had worked?

WWII Questions (continued):

11. What if Hitler had remained a democratic leader?
12. What if Britain and her allies had decided to stop Hitler sooner?
13. What if Hitler had honored the Munich Accords?
14. What if Hitler had not attacked Poland?
15. What if Appeasement had continued?
16. What if the Maginot Line had worked?
17. What if Dunkirk had failed?
18. What if the Axis powers had gotten control of Egypt and the Suez Canal?
19. What if Italy had surrendered sooner?
20. What if Mussolini had committed suicide?
21. What if Mussolini had successfully escaped to Germany?
22. What if Italy had not changed sides in the war?
23. What if Hitler had not attacked Russia?
24. What if Hitler had attacked Russia earlier in the summer?
25. What if Hitler had conquered Moscow?
26. What if Japan had attacked Russia instead of the US?
27. What if Stalin had not killed so many generals in the purges?
28. What if Stalin had surrendered?
29. What if the Germans had not tried to conquer Stalingrad?
30. What if the Germans had conquered the Baku oilfields?
31. What if some of the neutral countries like Spain had joined the war?
32. What if Hitler had had a better navy at the beginning of the war?
33. What if radar and sonar had not been invented?
34. What if the Germans had discovered the atomic bomb first?
35. What if the assassination attempt on Hitler had worked?
36. What if the Invasion of Normandy had taken place at an earlier or later time?
37. What if the Battle of the Bulge had succeeded in pushing back the Allies?
38. What if the Americans and British had conquered all of Germany before the Russians arrived?
39. What if Hitler had not committed suicide?
40. What if Japan had concentrated all of her strength on conquering China?
41. What if Japan had conquered Australia or India?
42. What if Japan had never attacked Pearl Harbor?
43. What if the US had been prepared for the attack on Pearl Harbor?
44. What if the attack on Pearl Harbor had succeeded in sinking all of the American aircraft carriers?
45. What if the US had decided to attack Japan directly instead of island hopping?
46. What if the atomic bomb had not been used on Japan?

WWII Questions (continued):

47. What if the atomic bomb had been used on Germany?
48. What if Japan still hadn't surrendered after the 2 atomic bombs were dropped?
49. What if the atomic bomb had been only been demonstrated, but not dropped on a city?
50. What if the atomic bomb had been used on a strictly military target?
51. What if there had been only one atomic bomb?
52. What if WWII had been resolved by means of a treaty like the Versailles Treaty following WWI with reparations, demilitarization, and loss of land from the defeated powers?

Cold War Questions:

1. What if Roosevelt had lived to finish his fourth term in office?
2. What if there had been no atomic bomb?
3. What if the hydrogen bomb had not been invented?
4. What if the US and USSR had remained allies?
5. What if Germany had remained united and neutral?
6. What if the Soviets had invented the atomic bomb first?
7. What if the Soviets had invented the hydrogen bomb first?
8. What if the Soviets had allowed free elections in Eastern Europe after WWII?
9. What if the Nationalists had won the Civil War in China?
10. What if Korea had been completely reunified by one side or the other?
11. What if China had stayed out of Korea?
12. What if Truman had allowed MacArthur to remain as the commander of Allied forces in Korea?
13. What if the Soviets had used combat troops in Korea?
14. What if the US had used the atomic bomb in North Korea?
15. What if the UN had been involved in Vietnam the same way that they were in Korea?
16. What if the United Nations had not been formed?
17. What if NATO or the Warsaw Pact had not been formed?
18. What if the Marshall Plan had not been implemented?
19. What if Sputnik had been a flop?
20. What if the USA had launched a satellite before Sputnik?
21. What if the Berlin Blockade had succeeded?
22. What if the US had intervened to aid the revolt in Hungary against Communism?
23. What if the United States had been Communist and the Russians were Capitalists?

Cold War Questions (continued):

24. What if Joseph McCarthy was right about there being Communists in the Army and the State Department?
25. What if Nixon had been president instead of Eisenhower?
26. What if Nixon had been president instead of Kennedy?
27. What if Fidel Castro had not become a Communist?
28. What if Eisenhower had been president instead of Kennedy during the Bay of Pigs invasion?
29. What if the Bay of Pigs invasion had worked?
30. What if the CIA's attempts to kill Fidel Castro had worked?
31. What if the Cuban Missile Crisis had actually turned into a full-scale war?
32. What if the US had attempted to invade Cuba during the Cuban Missile Crisis?
33. What if the Soviets had used the missiles in Cuba?
34. What if Kennedy had lived to finish his term in office? Would he have escalated our involvement in Vietnam to a full-scale war?
35. What if the US had invaded North Vietnam?
36. What if the US had used nuclear missiles on North Vietnam?
37. What if the Chinese and Soviets had not aided North Vietnam?
38. What if the US had not invaded Cambodia?
39. What if there had been no Ho Chi Minh?
40. What if there had been no Ho Chi Minh Trail?
41. What if the US had withdrawn from Vietnam earlier?
42. What if the US had never been involved in Vietnam?
43. What if there were still two Vietnam's today?
44. What if both sides had honored their obligations under the Paris Cease-Fire Agreements?
45. What if the Prague Spring had succeeded?
46. What if the Republic of Biafra had retained its independence?
47. What if Juan Peron had not married Evita?
48. What if Nixon had not gone to China?
49. What if the Great Leap Forward had worked?
50. What if the Cultural Revolution had worked?
51. What if China had been admitted to the United Nations earlier?
52. What if the Great Leap Forward had not occurred?
53. What if the Cultural Revolution had not occurred?
54. What if Mao had remained a Confucianist?
55. What if someone like Mao remained in charge of China today?
56. What if the Tiananmen Square Revolt had succeeded?
57. What if Britain had refused to return Hong Kong to China?
58. What if Argentina had won the Falklands War?
59. What if Ronald Reagan had been president in 1976?
60. What if Jimmy Carter had succeeded in rescuing the hostages in Iran?

Cold War Questions (continued):

61. What if the SALT II Treaty had been ratified?
62. What if the Soviets had succeeded in taking over Afghanistan?
63. What if Ronald Reagan had not proposed arms control talks with Soviets?
64. What if Ronald Reagan had not been willing to negotiate with Gorbachev?
65. What if Ronald Reagan had not increased arms spending in the early 1980's?
66. What if the Strategic Defense Initiative had been completed?
67. What if Mikhail Gorbachev had remained a Stalinist style of Communist?
68. What if Mikhail Gorbachev's reforms had worked?
69. What if the USSR had not broken apart? What would the world be like today?
70. What if the USSR had won the Cold War? What would the world be like today?
71. What if Boris Yeltsin had not forced Gorbachev out of power?
72. What if the Communist revolt against Gorbachev had worked?
73. What if the Berlin Wall had not come down?
74. What if Gorbachev had resisted Eastern Europe's attempts to no longer be Communist?
75. What if Eastern Europe had remained Communist?
76. What if Gorbachev had resisted the Baltic State's attempts to leave the USSR?
77. What if peace in the Middle East had been achieved?
78. What if Israel's enemies had succeeded in taking it over?
79. What if the US had decided not to do anything about Iraq's invasion of Kuwait?
80. What if the Persian Gulf had not contained oil?
81. What if George Bush had not been able to assemble the coalition of allies against Iraq?
82. What if Saddam Hussein had been killed in the Gulf War?
83. What if all of Iraq had been occupied during Desert Storm?
84. What if the US had decided not to do anything about the war in the Balkans?
85. What if Slobodan Milosovic had completed his campaign of ethnic cleansing in the Balkans?

About the author

Richard Di Giacomo graduated from San José State University with a BA in Ancient and Medieval history, a BA in Social Science and an MA in American History. He has been a teacher for 20 years and has taught in a variety of schools from private and continuation schools to public high schools. He has taught everything from at risk and limited English students to honors and college preparatory classes. The subjects he has taught include US and World History, Government, Economics, Bible and Ethics, History of the Cold War, and Contemporary World History.

He has been a reviewer and contributor to textbooks, and a frequent presenter at social studies conferences on the use of simulations, videos, and computers in education. Rich's love for role-playing and strategy games led him to develop his unique books which combine the open-ended outcomes of role-playing with the tough decisions made by people in times of historical crisis. Students often relate that these are their most memorable and enjoyable activities of the year. They bring history to life so vividly that students can't seem to stop talking about the simulations long after class is over!

How to contact the author:

It is my sincere hope that you will find these simulations as enjoyable, educational, and easy-to-use as I have. They are really unlike any other kind of simulation available in the market today. Should you feel like you need further information or suggestions as to how to run these simulations in your classroom, please contact me via e-mail at:

Krinibar@AOL.COM

or via US Mail at:

Richard Di Giacomo

2486 Aram Avenue

San Jose, California 95128 USA

Also by the same author:

Short Role-playing Simulations for US History Classrooms 3rd Edition © 2002

ISBN 0-9706237-1-2   17.50

With the following simulations:
1. Reconstruction Simulation
2. Taking Colonies
3. Great Powers Game (W.W.I)
4. Strike Simulation
5. W.W.II Debates
6. Cold War Simulation
7. Cuban Missile Crisis Simulation
8. Hippie Day
9. 20th Century Slang
10. US History Counterfactuals: "What if...?" Questions

Short Role-playing Simulations for Middle School World History

By Richard Di Giacomo
1st Edition © 2006

ISBN 0-9706237-4-7   17.50

With the following simulations:

1. Archaeology Lab: Excavate Your School!
2. Invent Your Own Writing System
3. The Mesopotamian Trade Game
4. Monument to a Pharaoh Competition
5. Colonies of the Ancient Mediterranean
6. Roman Soldiers' Letters Home
7. Roman Emperor Simulation
8. The Mandate of Heaven: The Chinese Dynasty Game
9. Make Your Own Illuminated Manuscript
10. Crusader Job Interview
11. Medieval Conversation
12. Christopher Columbus Trial
13. World History Counterfactuals: "What if?"

and...
THE INFLUENCE OF RENAISSANCE HUMANISM ON THE EXPLORERS OF THE ITALIAN ERA OF DISCOVERY

By Richard Di Giacomo

© 1991 All Rights Reserved   ISBN 09706237-2-0   15.95

US History Activities for English Language Learners

2nd Edition © 2007

If you have been having a hard time finding quality social studies subject area activities for English language learners, your search is over!

This book contains several engaging activities that teach both the content area of Early US History and English language development skills. ISBN 09706237-5-5 15.95

The activities inside include:
- games
- letter writing
- cloze activities
- bingo
- total physical response
- vocabulary context clues
- historical newspapers
- quotations
- political cartoons
- idioms and slang
- speech-writing
- writing a children's book
- note taking strategies
- oral history
- role-playing
- grammar editing
- group decision-making
- graphic organizers
- and many other activities!

To put a little fun in your classroom try:

The History Teacher's Joke Book

A sample of the torture in store for your students:

Danny: "I like the mammals in Tasmania."
Annie: "You devil, you!"

Maureen: "Did you get to see much of Virginia?"
Doreen: "No, Chesapeake."

Ed: "What do you do if your food store flops in India?"
Fred: "Open a New Delhi."

Teacher: "Sometimes pharaohs died quite young."
Student: "Tut, tut, what a shame!"

Apollo: "Which ancient battle had the best lunch meat?"
Vulcan: "The Battle of Salamis."

Teacher: "Can an obscure figure from a small Mediterranean island become the Emperor of all France?"
Class: "Of Corsican!"

Teacher: "Why did Theodore Roosevelt drop out of politics?"
Smart Alec: "Because Teddy could bear no more."

Teacher: "What was the British response to the German trenches in WWI?
Pupil: "Tanks a lot!"

Mitch: "Why does the Dalai Lama go to Las Vegas?"
Rich: "He loves Tibet!"

ISBN 0-9706237-3-9   8.50

The History Teacher's Movie Guide
Choosing and Using the Right Films for Your Classroom

By Richard Di Giacomo

This book helps you get good films that are free from bias, anachronisms, or objectionable content.
There are many great tips on how to use films more effectively in your classroom and interesting assignments to go with them.

Magnifico Publications 2486 Aram Avenue, San José, Ca. 95128

http://www.magnificopublications.com   ISBN 09706237-7-1   17.50

Magnifico Publications Order Form

HOW TO ORDER
(1) Order our books through our web page at http://www.magnificopublications.com.
(2) Order them through the following web pages: Social Studies School Services. http://catalog.socialstudies.com/c/@FcDiHj_IWo0jw/Pages/list.html?nocache@8+curList@0. Teachers' Discovery. http://www.teachersdiscovery.com. Amazon.com. http://www.amazon.com/exec/obidos/tg/stores/detail/-/books/0970623704/reviews/qid%3D996735781/sr%3D1-2/ref%3Dsc%5Fb%5F2/104-9864913-9328725.
(3) Contact Magnifico Publications directly at 408-286-5179 or E-mail us at krinibar@aol.com.
(4) Mail this order form to: *Magnifico Publications* 2486 Aram Ave. San Jose, CA. 95128.

Name_____

School or Organization_____

Department: _____

Address_____

City_____ State_____
ZIP_____Country_____
E-Mail Address_____Phone (____)_____

Ship to:			
Title(s):		# ordered	cost
ISBN 09706237-1-2	*Role-playing Simulations for US History Classrooms*		17.50
ISBN 09706237-5-5	*US History Activities for English Language Learners*		15.95
ISBN 09706237-0-4	*Role-playing Simulations for World History Classrooms*		17.50
ISBN 09706237-2-0	*The New Man and the New World: The Influence of Renaissance Humanism on the Explorers of the Italian Era of Discovery*		15.95
ISBN 09706237-3-9	*The History Teacher's Joke Book*		8.50
ISBN 0-9706237-4-7	*Short Role-playing Simulations for Middle School World History*		17.50
ISBN 09706237-7-1	*The History Teacher's Movie Guide*		17.50
ISBN 09706237-6-3	*Ohlone Teacher's Resource*		30.00
		Shipping & handling	4.50
		Tax (CA only)	
		Total cost	